CHRISTIAN UNITY

# CHRISTIAN UNITY

## A CATHOLIC VIEW

Being an account of the first official conference
organized by the Bishops' Committee for
Christian Unity (Heythrop August 1962)

*Edited by*

### JOHN C. HEENAN
**Archbishop of Liverpool**

## SHEED AND WARD
### LONDON AND NEW YORK

FIRST PUBLISHED 1962
SHEED AND WARD, LTD
33 MAIDEN LANE
LONDON W.C.2
AND
SHEED AND WARD, INC
64 UNIVERSITY PLACE
NEW YORK 3

*This book is set in 11 on 12 pt. Baskerville*

*Made and printed in Great Britain by*
*W. & J. Mackay & Co. Ltd., Chatham*

# CONTENTS

# 1. HOW THE HEYTHROP CONFERENCE CAME ABOUT

*Archbishop Heenan*

A FEW days after the Heythrop Conference I was invited to lay the foundation stone of a Cistercian abbey in Northern Ireland. The occasion was to be marked by an open-air Pontifical Mass at which I was to preach. I had been invited by the Abbot because of my membership of the Secretariat for Promoting Christian Unity. After an unpromising start the monks had now made friends with most of the Protestant farmers in the neighbourhood. The Abbot expected many Protestants at the function.

You may be sure that I prepared my sermon with more than usual care. It is well known that religious relations in Northern Ireland are delicate. Feeling, even in the recent past, has run deep. It seemed right and, indeed, obvious for me to tell my mixed audience of the new friendship which has sprung up elsewhere in these islands. I urged them to remember above all that they were brothers in Christ. I told them that being a Christian is more important than being Catholic or Protestant. I was not intending to enunciate any theological principle but merely to encourage friendship between Christians whose hostility has caused nothing but harm in the history of Ireland.

On my return to England I was surprised at the

reaction of some Catholics to my sermon, which had been widely reported. Some well-educated Catholics were apparently quite shocked by my words. I select three letters which give their point of view. It is an illusion to think that the average Catholic is yearning to identify himself with his non-Catholic brethren. The overwhelming majority of Catholics as yet has little interest in the Ecumenical Movement. The story of reactionary bishops restraining their eager flocks from contact with the separated brethren is largely a myth. The first letter came from a lady living in the country:

I have read today in *The Times* that you said "This new spirit has been created because Christians have come to realize that what matters most is not that they are Catholic or Protestant but that they are fellow Christians."

My heart sank when I read this because if it is true then why have I, my husband and many converts who have sacrificed so much in order to become Catholics ever bothered to do so? How much easier for us all to have remained Christians, as it were, in the Church of England—where life in this present age is made so easy with divorce and birth control being allowed and no discipline being exercised—if that is what matters most. Your words may very well cause converts, especially among the young, to slip back into the Protestant church and give up their Faith. Our young

family have had to fight hard for theirs and
your remarks will not make it easier for them.
Surely what we need now is more encouragement to hold the true Faith and more clear
exposition of the reasons for the truth of the
Catholic Church and the untruth of the Protestant churches.

Incidentally, I see today that in their New
Testament they are intending to leave out the
word "Virgin" in Isaias' prophecy which will
lead, as it already has among modern churchmen, to a repudiation of the Virgin Birth. Are
these the Christians with whom we are to cultivate a precious new friendship and that it is to
matter most that we should be one with them
than that we should be Catholics and belong to
the one true Church? For what did our martyrs
suffer torture and agonizing death if what mat-
tered most was that they should be Christians
whether Catholic or Protestant? But *The Times*
does misquote and I hope that this may be the
case on this occasion.

The next letter is from a priest in the south of
England:

May I bring to your notice the enclosed
cutting from *The Times* of today, with deep
respect and humility? The plain common-sense
meaning to ordinary men and women can only
be that to be a Christian is something other than
and over and above being "Catholic" or "Protestant", and it is time we put that something

first . . . whatever *branch* of the Christian Church we belong to.

This is precisely what my Anglican neighbours in this very staunch and intelligently Anglican area want to be told, and I have no doubt I shall get this remark back from them in a short time. It is surely most confusing for the average good Catholic boy or girl, it makes for indifferentism, prevents conversions, and offers no reason why any little girl should belong to a branch of the Church of Christ which is so very old-fashioned and stiff about birth control for instance. I do realize that what one actually said is not what appears in the public press, but there has been a certain amount of this kind of reporting also in the Catholic Press of late, and one wonders if it is necessary to so devalue the word "Catholic" as synonymous with "Christian" in order to restore mutual friendship between Catholic and Protestant? Anyhow, the Fathers of the Church always did their best to avoid just that way of speaking.

The most trenchant letter came from a layman:

For long now, if I may be permitted to say so, I have been an admirer of the utterances of your Grace, both in speech and in print. It was, therefore, with the added shock of surprise, that I read, this morning, a newspaper report of a speech made by your Grace in Northern Ireland, and I can only assume that the speech has been misreported. Your Grace is reported as having said: "This new spirit has been created because Christians have come to realize that what matters most is not that they are Catholics or Protestants, but that they are fellow Christians."

For my own part, I have not come to realize any such thing. I am, and I remain, a Catholic because I believe that only the Catholic Church is in possession of the truth, and for me, that alone is sufficient to make Catholicism matter infinitely more than a realization that many non-Catholics are Christians. If other creeds reject, as they do, part of Catholic truth they must, of necessity, be in error. It is because of this that I pray for my separated brethren who are, at present, denied a gift that has been given to me. And because I can hear Mass every day in peace, I have a sense of gratitude and obligation to those men of the sixteenth and seventeenth centuries who made that possible because they were content to suffer a barbarous death at the hands of their "fellow Christians" rather than accept a religion which they knew to be untrue; they, at least, had no thought that fellowship in Christianity was more important than their Catholic Faith, and they would have indignantly rejected any such idea.

Since I find it hard to distinguish the statement attributed to Your Grace from that "indifferentism" against which we have all been warned, I should, as a devoted admirer of Your Grace, welcome an assurance that your words have been misreported.

I cannot tell to what extent the sentiments expressed by my correspondents represent the lay attitude to the Ecumenical Movement. But from experience I know that many Catholics, doubtless because it is still so new, feel uneasy about the whole idea. Although there are Catholic enthusiasts, especially in academic circles, the fact is that Catholics in England are far less interested than, for example, the Catholics of Germany, in Christian co-operation. It is sometimes alleged that the chief reason is lack of leadership. It is true that the English Hierarchy has not yet made many public moves to extend ecumenical work. It is important to discover why. It is a modern delusion that without publicity nothing useful can ever be achieved.

It has been said that English Catholics disapprove of what Christians are doing elsewhere in Europe and that, in fact, they are reluctant to follow the lead given by Pope John. In support of this accusation it is recalled that little was ever heard in this country of the Instruction on the Ecumenical Movement given by the Holy Office in 1949.

It is true that the Catholic Church abroad was much quicker to act upon the Holy Office Instruction. We shall see, later on, the reason why it is so much easier for the Ecumenical Movement to make progress on the Continent. It is important to be aware, meanwhile, that Instructions from the Holy Office are normally issued not to the faithful nor even to the clergy but directly to the bishops.

The bishop is described in canon law as the Ordinary (*Ordinarius Loci*). He is presumed to understand local conditions and the special needs of his own people. That is why the Holy Office leaves to the Ordinary the time and manner in which its Instructions are carried out. From experience the Holy See knows that its general directions must be interpreted by the bishops, whom "the Holy Ghost hath placed . . . to rule the Church of God". (Acts 20. 28.)

It now seems providential that the bishops were in no hurry to initiate widespread ecumenical activity. The ecumenical task can be undertaken today with a prospect of success largely lacking ten years ago. The improvement in relations between Catholics and other Christians has been rapid and far-reaching. It is true that co-operation in social work has been on the increase for at least a quarter of a century, but this kind of united action is very different from a theological encounter which is of the essence of true ecumenical dialogue.

The eager desire for friendship among Christians of all denominations is now so manifest and genuine that we easily forget that we are still only in the courtship stage. Being determined never again to return to the hostility of the past, we are apt to conceal even from ourselves the fact that it is a very recent past. The public memory is notoriously short. No small effort is required to recall the religious atmosphere of even a decade ago. I propose to recall it not in order to open old wounds but only to stress the wisdom of religious leaders of all denominations in Britain who have moved with caution in the ecumenical field.

I shall describe subsequently the rapid growth of good relations in recent months and years. But we must first try to recapture the atmosphere of an earlier phase. In the most critical days of the Second World War Pope Pius XII was recognized on all sides as ideally placed to raise the issue of peace. Not being a citizen of any secular state, the Pope could not reasonably be suspected of speaking for only one of the contending parties. If the initiative had been taken by a bishop in England or Germany, almost certainly his action would have been misconstrued even by his own country-men. It is not hard to imagine, for example, the kind of reception an appeal from the Archbishop of Canterbury would have received. The enemy would have called him the mouthpiece of Churchill. His own people might well have accused him of the then popular crime of appease-ment.

Pope Pius XII, in the event, appealed to the nations at war to stop further bloodshed. He pro-posed five peace points as a basis for negotiations. This papal action was welcomed in Great Britain by Christians of every denomination.

As a result, a remarkable letter in support of the Pope's appeal appeared in *The Times* over the signatures of Dr. Lang, Archbishop of Canterbury, Cardinal Hinsley, Archbishop of Westminster, the Rev. W. Armstrong, Moderator of the Free

Church Federal Council, and Dr. Temple, Archbishop of York. Thus the first chapter in the modern history of religious co-operation in this country was honourably written.

Even more striking evidence of the desire among Christians to co-operate was soon to come. Cardinal Hinsley had formed an organization which he called The Sword of the Spirit. Its object was to prepare the way for a new social order after the establishment of peace in Europe. Although it was part of what was called Catholic Action, The Sword of the Spirit specialized in arranging common Christian platforms. Its rallies and meetings normally advertised, in addition to a Catholic speaker, an Anglican and a representative of the Free Churches.

Christians whom tradition in this country had hitherto restrained from united action in public eagerly sought in the Pope's peace points grounds for further co-operation. It was universally felt that united witness, however restricted, was a sufficient novelty to arouse interest even among non-religious citizens. Since all denominations had recorded their agreement with the Pope's outline of the social justice to be sought after the war, it was agreed to attempt to permeate the country with the spirit of *The Times* letter. It was held that Catholics and Protestants, however divided in theology, could unite sincerely in working for justice and peace in the post-war world. The first and most spectacular joint witness was given to London from the stage of the Stoll Theatre during

the weekend of May 10th and 11th, 1941. On the
Saturday Cardinal Hinsley presided. The Luft-
waffe chose that night to carry out its most
indiscriminate bombing raid on London and thus
advertised the urgency of Christian unity against
barbarism. The next day, despite the almost insuperable difficulty of travel through bomb
damage, the vast hall was once again crowded.
This time it was to hear the Archbishop of
Canterbury. From the Saturday meeting thousands
were turned away. But this was less remarkable
than the fact of any meeting being held on the
Sunday in the conditions then prevailing in
London.

After submitting to the meeting the resolution
of supporting the Pope's peace points, Cardinal
Hinsley ended his address with these words:

> Our unity must not be in sentiment and in
> word only; it must be carried into practical
> measures. Let us have a regular system of con-
> sultation and co-operation from now onwards,
> such as His Lordship the Bishop of Chichester
> [Dr. Bell] has suggested, to agree on a plan of
> action which shall win the peace when the din
> of battle is ended.

The Stoll meetings were followed by similar
demonstrations in many parts of the country.
Christians abandoned their former mutual suspicions. They made united efforts to present a
Christian front to the enemy in Europe and to the
indifferent at home. But despite good will and

enthusiasm this close unity did not long survive. The gladiators began to dispute about the ownership of The Sword of the Spirit. There is no need to retell the story here. It is sufficient to say that it was found advisable for Catholics to retain control of The Sword of the Spirit while other Christians united in an organization known as Religion and Life. There was no open quarrel among the leaders but misunderstandings arose and prudent men on both sides realized that *Festina lente* is the safest rule of the road to Christian unity.

During the War, danger of invasion and the suffering caused by air-raids drew together men and women of all classes and of every religion. The unity of the people and their mutual compassion made England a pleasant land although it was badly scarred. But when danger had passed citizens inevitably began once more to seek their interests in their own social circle or religious body. The old divisions and bitterness were not renewed, but the new-found fellowship did not mature. The successors of Cardinal Hinsley, Archbishop Lang and Archbishop Temple were preoccupied with responsibilities within their own communities. Christian co-operation on any large scale did not long survive the war.

Even before the end of the war divergence of interests had begun to appear. We may mention as an example the Education Act of 1944. This put a strain upon relations between Christians that has only recently been relaxed. The Catholic community was appalled at the financial burden

which the proposed reorganization of schools
would entail. They felt aggrieved that while so
many young fathers of families were away fighting
for freedom the politicians wanted to introduce a
controversial educational system.

It proved impossible to find any joint educational programme in which Anglicans and Nonconformists were willing to co-operate with their
Catholic friends. Other Christians did not, for the
most part, share the anxiety of Catholics. The
Church of England had grown accustomed,
through force of circumstances, to allowing many
of its schools to pass to the control of the Local
Education Authority. The Nonconformists had
satisfied their needs by erecting large halls, and
they had not built schools for more than a generation. Catholics, therefore, once more felt isolated,
and in the campaign for what they held to be
justice were rarely able to induce other Christians
to share a common platform. Some Anglicans were,
of course, strong supporters of church schools,
but usually Catholics had to fight alone. This fact
must be recalled in the context of the Ecumenical
Movement because it was one factor leading many
English Catholics to doubt if Christian co-operation could ever become more than an empty
gesture.

It has been wisely said—and in these pages it
will be repeated—that true unity among Christians
involves theology. This is agreed by theologians of
every school. Joint action to promote social justice
or to relieve human suffering can be undertaken

not only by Protestants with Catholics but by
Christians with Jews, Moslems or, indeed, atheists.
This is admirable, but if something deeper than
humanitarian action is envisaged by Christian
unity, a theological dialogue must eventually be
undertaken.

Theologians, however, when they speak of
theology almost always mean dogmatic theology
and the study of Sacred Scripture. They naturally
tend to concentrate on pure theology and, so far,
have made few attempts to discuss ethics and
moral theology. This is one reason why scholars
experience less difficulty than the pastors and
people in establishing close relations with those of
other faiths. The kind of question they consider is
often remote from the practical problems of co-
operation met by the average priest. Christendom,
in early centuries, was split by disagreement among
theologians regarding the nature of Christ and the
procession of the Holy Spirit. The battle later
raged around the meaning of grace, free will and
justification. Theologians still have abundant
material for their dialogues—the Word of God, for
example, inspiration, the Eucharist and the nature
of the Church. Such subjects today can usually be
discussed without heat. But the more human problems still arouse strong emotions—for instance,
the demands made by the Catholic Church before
granting a dispensation for a mixed marriage.
Church discipline affecting the behaviour of individuals and families naturally makes the delicacy
of the ecumenical dialogue much more apparent.

There is, indeed, wide disagreement among Christians over the meaning and extent of the natural law. Catholic teaching on divorce, sterilization, euthanasia, abortion and artificial birth-prevention is not on a par with the purely ecclesiastical laws forbidding meat on Fridays or requiring celibacy in the clergy. Divergence of view in moral theology will, of course, eventually be taken into consideration by those engaged in the dialogue. It is, moreover, much more present to clergy and lay Christians than the problems which hitherto have exercised the minds of theologians.

It is important to take note of these difficulties before looking at the more hopeful prospects for Christian unity. Emotionally, all good Christians want to tear down without delay all barriers between them. But emotion is a poor guide to truth. To speak as if no substantial obstacles separate Christians would be to promote an indifferentism which might destroy all religious convictions. The laity would become bewildered and disillusioned. Christians must not be led faster than they are willing to travel on the road to unity. Due account must be taken of those sincere Protestants who are still uneasy about having contact of any kind with Rome. Some Catholics still need to be reassured that the Church has no thought of abandoning her claim to be the one true Church. They are dismayed when told that it has become offensive to talk about the *return* of the separated brethren.

The movement towards Christian unity is still

in its early stages. But the progress has already been quite remarkable. Those who, in all sincerity, used to attack each other's views now, with equal sincerity, resist the temptation to denounce and seek rather to understand. About ten years ago, for example, two Anglican bishops, who are now my friends, publicly described Communism and Roman Catholicism as totalitarian systems equally harmful to Christianity. What my friends then objected to in the Church of Rome they doubtless still find objectionable. But they now realize, as do we all, that fuller understanding of the other side leads to a new outlook.

It is not surprising, in view of the religious history of our country, that approaches on both sides should have been tentative and hesitant. Having suffered so much from each other, Christians have been reluctant to risk the further hurt of rebuff. Less than fifty years ago, after all, Catholics and Protestants in England used to denounce each other almost as part of their religious duty. On the Continent, too, there have been quarrels between Christians, but the origins of their disagreement have been rather different from our own. Abroad, the Old Faith has been much more clearly different from the religion of the Churches of the Reform. The Reformed Churches, while claiming to be part of the Catholic Church, do not regard themselves as the successors of the medieval Church. In most places there was no "takeover bid" by the Reformers.

Retaining possession of their cathedrals,

churches and universities, Continental Catholics
have a self-confidence which is only gradually
returning to English Catholics. Foreigners often
think of English Catholics as obsessed by what
happened at Tyburn. Catholics are in fact much
more conscious of the results of the Reformation in
England. Religious suppression followed a much
more tortuous and prolonged path here than
abroad. It was, after all, only in the last century
that certain elementary rights were restored to
Catholic citizens. It is not surprising, therefore,
that it has proved more difficult to establish close
ecumenical contact between Catholics and non-
Catholics in this country.

The fact that the old cathedrals, parish churches,
universities and old schools are part of the Establishment has made English Catholics look like outsiders. Nobody can wonder if Protestants have
traditionally regarded as arrogant the Catholic
claim to be the genuine *Ecclesia Anglicana*. Possession, after all, is regarded as nine points of the law.
This kind of complication does not arise in France
or Germany. The Reformed Churches repudiated
the medieval Church. There was no question of
the validity of priestly orders; no Oxford Movement; no Newman; no significant defection by
Protestant clergy; no vast Catholic immigration.
But these facts of history make relations between
Catholics and other Christians in England and
Wales delicate beyond the imagination of Christians abroad.

That is why it would have been foolish for

Catholic bishops and leaders of other religious bodies in this country to emulate Christians on the Continent. Our history makes it imperative for us to conduct the ecumenical movement in our own way. Mutual trust has grown so fast that we shall soon, by God's grace, be as much at ease with each other as Continental Catholics and Protestants. The non-Catholics will not feel the need to go abroad to establish a dialogue with Catholics. There will be more English Catholic scholars and less insistence on past grievances. Both Catholics and Protestants will be more ready to deplore (and forget!) the crimes committed in the name of religion.

Catholics and non-Catholics have come much closer in every way. At the beginning of the century religious divisions were much sharper. Christians called themselves either Protestant or Catholic. There was an undertone of loyalty in the term "Protestant" and something alien about the Catholic title. Except in the North, Catholics were few and, apart from the old families, they were mostly Irish or converts. Few Catholics received a first-class education, and fewer still went to a university. All these facts need to be taken into consideration if we are to understand why the pace of Christian co-operation has been slow in this country.

Another event of a quite different order greatly helped to foster friendship between Catholics and Protestants abroad. It would be an exaggeration to call Adolf Hitler the father of Continental ecumenicism, but no man has been more

responsible for throwing Catholics and Protestants into each other's arms. In Germany and
the Nazi-occupied territories of Europe, Christians united to resist the new paganism. It was
impossible not to realize that their Christian
allegiance counted in this life-and-death struggle
far more than denominational loyalty. They really
were fighting a battle for survival. If Hitler had
won the war, Christianity would today be no
better off in the West than it is in the East. In
opposition to the Nazis Christians sought every
opportunity of helping each other—and, to their
great credit, of helping the hapless Jews. They
fought each other's battles and even used each
other's churches. Small wonder that when the war
ended Catholics and Protestants emerged as true
brothers. If we had suffered enemy occupation in
England I have no doubt that the ecumenical
movement would be now much further advanced.

There is yet another reason why Catholics in
this country have not been able to move so fast as
their brethren abroad. Still the Church of the
poor, we are only now beginning to have impressive numbers among the educated. We have
not lost touch with the workers. Most priests and
bishops, in any case, are of working-class origin.
Because few Catholics have been in a position to
follow higher studies, ecumenical work was
necessarily slow. It is not a question of one law
for the educationally rich and another for the
educationally poor. It is a question of not giving
scandal to those who would be shocked by ecu-

menical actions which are perfectly safe on an academic level. Scholars rather tend to shrug off scandal of the weak as unimportant. The bishops, however, must be on their guard against giving scandal to simple members of the flock. But the Hierarchy, although acting cautiously, has not been inactive. It did little enough about the Holy Office Instruction in 1949, but this has proved to have been fortunate.

During the last two years the bishops have given a great deal of thought to planning the extension of ecumenical work in this country. One of the first actions of the Hierarchy was to establish a Bishops' Committee for Christian Unity. This was the first of its kind in Europe, and soon afterwards the French Hierarchy founded a committee on the English model. Some complain that progress towards Christian unity has been culpably slow. I am not at all sure, in view of our traditional difficulties, that progress has not been satisfactory. I am sure, in any case, that in view of the old enmities, Christian unity might have remained no more than a pious expression until the end of the century, had not Cardinal Roncalli ascended the papal throne as John XXIII.

It is not easy to say what it was about Pope John that led him to be immediately and universally acclaimed. From the beginning of his reign everybody spoke of him with affection. Yet he lacks the qualities which usually make a Pope renowned—he is not an eminent scholar or linguist or diplomat, as were some of his recent predecessors. He has been admired not for his gifts but for himself. He is the Common Father and interprets that fatherhood in the widest sense. No-one can find in him a trace of narrowness or intolerance.

Non-Catholics were not slow to discover what kind of man had become Pope. The more they heard about him the more they were attracted. Even his casual actions became news and won him new friends. He went to the city gaol because, as he said, the prisoners could not come out to see him. When he heard that an old friend or a loyal worker from Vatican City was dying he would go out to pay a visit. He chided the *Osservatore Romano*, the Vatican newspaper, for always describing him as "the August Pontiff". "Why not just call me 'the Pope' or 'the Holy Father'?" he asked. He did not like to see retainers at the Vatican genuflecting every time they came near him. He told them to genuflect, if they must, when they met him in the morning and then have done with it for the rest of the day. This was the kind of news people loved to hear about the new Pope.

What had all this to do with Christian unity? It had a great deal to do with it, because although Pope John did not invent the idea, it was he who quickened the pulse of the whole movement. His evident sincerity and love for all Christians gave a new meaning to the ecumenical dialogue between the theologians. It is possible, after all, to conduct the dialogue on a purely intellectual level. But religion is a question of the heart as well as of the mind.

One of the first men to give a practical response to the gesture of Pope John was Dr. Fisher, then Archbishop of Canterbury. He has told me that before the coming of Pope John he had decided to visit the Orthodox Patriarchs before retiring from Canterbury. It had naturally not entered his head to include the Holy Father in his round of farewell visits. But, captured by the Pope's love for his fellow Christians, Dr. Fisher decided to pay his call of courtesy.

Rarely has an act of courtesy been so richly or so quickly rewarded. Courtesy is, perhaps, too weak a word. Courtesy, after all, is a form of charity, and true charity never fails to warm all who come within its radius. It would be wrong to say that good feeling between Christians began only after the famous visit to the Vatican. But it is true that after the visit relations between Anglicans and Catholics can never be quite the same. Since that time a bigot has come to be regarded as rather a bounder.

In announcing the Second Vatican Council Pope John made specific mention of Christian unity. To many he gave the impression that the great objective of the Council was to be reunion. But it soon became clear that the hope of Pope John is that through a renewal of spiritual life within the Church the way to reunion will be prepared.

To this end the Pope set up the Secretariat for Promoting Christian Unity. Its twofold task was to gather information likely to be useful to the Fathers of the Council and to keep the separated brethren informed of what steps towards unity the Church was taking. The Pope appointed Cardinal Bea to be President of the Secretariat. The Cardinal is known to scholars as one of the greatest living authorities on Sacred Scripture. For many years he was Rector of the Biblical Institute in Rome. But his attainments are not only intellectual. For long he has been a recognized master of the spiritual life. Pope Pius XII, in fact, chose him as father confessor. Cardinal Bea, a Jesuit and a German, has been accustomed to treat scriptural scholars of whatever country or religion as his brothers. He is familiar with their work as they are with his. In almost the literal sense, they spoke each other's language.

It would have been impossible, therefore, for Pope John to have found any cardinal more suited to take charge of the Secretariat for Promoting Christian Unity. Cardinal Bea has a compassion and breadth of view second only to that of Pope John himself. The members of the Secretariat were chosen personally by the Pope from among bishops and theologians of more than a dozen nations. These have met at intervals of about three months since 1960 to prepare schemes for submission to the Vatican Council.

In October 1961 the Bishops' Committee for Christian Unity announced its plan for the coming year. The first project was the Heythrop Conference. The bishops and the superiors of religious congregations were invited to send two representatives to Heythrop to study the pastoral and social approach to Christian Unity. It was decided to invite Cardinal Bea to direct the discussions.

The Hierarchy's committee was of the opinion that this first conference should be restricted to priests delegated by their superiors. It would have been unwise just yet to organize a wider conference to include non-Catholic theologians and Catholic laymen. Since most priests are still inexperienced in ecumenical work it was decided to make the conference a teaching conference. Priests were to be encouraged to speak what was in their minds and hearts. They were to listen and learn in order to carry back from the conference fresh information for their colleagues.

The Heythrop Conference is intended to be only a beginning. There will be, later on, opportunities for the laity to take a fuller share in ecumenical work. Dialogues with theologians belonging to other denominations have already been initiated by the Hierarchy. But these, of course, would not succeed if they were given publicity.

To call the Heythrop Conference interesting would be a masterly understatement. To some of the younger clergy taking part it was more like a revelation. Only the theologians at the conference knew the full extent to which the Ecumenical Movement has advanced in other countries. The papers, as the reader will see, were of an exceptionally high standard. Of these papers only Cardinal Bea's should be taken as authoritative.

He alone had the right to speak for the Holy See. The other papers were designed and intended to stimulate discussion. The writers of the papers are, of course, well read in their subjects. But they were invited not mainly to give theological lectures, but to kindle enthusiasm among priests with little experience of ecumenical work.

In this the lectures were highly successful. The priests freely expressed their opinion as to what policy should be followed by the Catholic Church in this country. It is agreeable to be able to record that during the week of discussions no word of criticism was made of the separated brethren. The priests were concerned to discover the short-comings of Catholics, but not to sit in judgement upon their non-Catholic friends. A full report of the discussions was sent to each bishop for study before the next meeting of the Hierarchy.

Although no report can be given here of the actual discussions, it may be of interest to record what some of the theologians had to say about joint prayer among Christians. They maintained that joint prayer, while highly regarded as a symbol of Christian unity, can easily become an obstacle. This view is apparently shared by Protestants of various denominations. The General Secretary of the World Council of Churches, for example, once said that divisions among Christians do not become less scandalous when concealed by ecu-menical varnish. Those experienced in the ecumenical field find that co-operation in social work and prayer in common easily become a substitute for real Christian unity. It is regarded by leading ecumenicists as dangerous to mask the urgency of facing differences in doctrine which are the chief reasons for a divided Christendom.

It is excellent that Christians and, indeed, men of any faith, should work together to help those in distress. World Refugee Year is a splendid example of what co-operation can achieve. But ecumenical experts insist that Christian leaders all too easily allow such co-operation to become the main objective of the whole movement. Individual members of the World Council of Churches discuss among themselves the advantage of joint eucharistic celebration. It is significant that many regard abstention from Holy Communion as even more important than any attempt at a joint service. The Eucharist, they say, is traditionally the symbol of unity. There is, therefore, no better way of bringing home manifestly and forcefully the disunity among Christians than by refraining from a common Communion table. This gives some idea of the importance of the ecumenical dialogue. Fundamentally divisions among Christians are a question of theology.

I wish it were possible to reproduce for the reader the spirit of the Heythrop Conference. It was more like a retreat than a week of study. Each priest began the day by celebrating Holy Mass. Some wondered privately, if after the Vatican Council such an occasion will be marked by concelebration. This is one of the many secrets which will not be disclosed until the Council has made its decisions. Each day ended with Benediction of the Most Blessed Sacrament.

The advertised programme included a lecture by Mgr. Willebrands on the scope and nature of the work being done in Rome by the Secretariat for Promoting Christian Unity. Unfortunately, he was unable to come to Oxford, because it was thought undesirable for the Cardinal and himself both to be absent from Rome at a time so close to the Council. Instead of substituting another lecture, the priests spent the extra time in chapel. There they enjoyed one of the richest spiritual experiences of the whole week. The venerable Cardinal celebrated a Dialogue Mass for Christian unity, and all the bishops and priests made the responses.

The Cardinal had come to Heythrop the bearer of a letter from the Vatican. The Holy Father, intensely interested in the conference, had instructed his Cardinal Secretary of State to convey his good wishes to all taking part.

Here is the text of the letter from the Vatican:

SECRETARIAT OF STATE

OF

HIS HOLINESS

Vatican City

July 26th 1962.

My Lord Archbishop,

The Holy Father has been informed of the Ecumenical Meeting of the secular and religious clergy of Great Britain which is shortly to be held at Heythrop College, and He has kindly directed me to convey His paternal greetings to Your Grace and to the assembly.

His Holiness bids me say that He was greatly pleased to learn of this meeting which Your Grace's zeal has prompted you to organize on the approach of the Second Vatican Council, and He cherishes the prayerful hope that it may be productive of much spiritual fruit.

This meeting of the priests of Great Britain might well derive inspiration and guidance from the words of St. Paul, "Veritatem facientes in charitate." While clergy and laity must adhere absolutely to all the truths of their Catholic faith and show firmness and loyalty in propounding them, at the same time they must practise the maximum of charity, in accordance with the admonition of the Apostle. (Cfr. 1 Cor. 13.) Therefore, endowed with genuine humility, they should show respect and regard for their separated brethren, treat them with benevolence and render them assistance wherever possible.

The Pontiff fervently invokes the enlightenment of the Holy Spirit upon the deliberations and discussions of this meeting, and, as a pledge of the copious spiritual fruit which He ardently hopes will result therefrom, He cordially imparts to Your Grace and to the assembled clergy His paternal Apostolic Blessing.

Gladly do I renew to Your Grace the

C.U.—B

assurance of my high esteem, and, with cordial
personal regards, I remain,

                    Yours sincerely in Christ,
                            A. G. Card. Cicognani.

At the end of the conference, led by Cardinal
Bea, the priests chanted a solemn Te Deum. The
Cardinal then gave the papal blessing. The greatest
lesson of the Heythrop Conference was the need for
prayer. The success of the campaign for Christian
unity does not depend on the learning or wit of the
theologians taking part in the dialogue. Success in
this, as in all spiritual enterprises, depends on the
grace of God.

There has been constant reference in these pages
to the Anglicans and little note of other religious
bodies. The reason is very simple. It was decided
that since so many attending the conference were
novices in ecumenical work it would be wise to
keep the issues as uncomplicated as possible. In
future conferences exclusive consideration will be
given to the Methodists, for example, or Baptists.
For those occasions experts in the theologies concerned will be on hand to guide the discussions. It
would be a pity if non-Anglicans were to think that
Catholics have interest only in members of the
Established Church. It is true that externally we
have more in common with episcopal Churches,
but all Christians are our concern. We cherish all
united to us by belief in God and love of his Son.

The outcome of the Vatican Council and the
future of the Ecumenical Movement are equally

in the hands of God. It is the duty of Christians to pray that God will guide both the Council and the Movement. Only God can remove from the hearts of his children pettiness and bitterness. Only God can give us a true love for the brotherhood. It is to foster this love and disclose the enlightened interest which Catholics in this country are showing in the work for Christian unity that this present volume has been published.

# 2. THE EIRENIC DIALOGUE

*Henry St. John, O.P.*

THE word "Eirenic" in the title of the lecture will have caught your eye. To be eirenic, and to enter into eirenic dialogue with our separated brethren, is to look first for the truth we hold in common, to understand where we are at *one*, and in the light of that to try to see, without rancour, what the differences between us really are. Our concern is the restoration of divided Christians to unity, the unity that Christ has given, and that we possess; and so our eyes are on the growing *desire* for unity, which is world-wide among divided Christians of every sort, and we are concerned with how we can integrate ourselves into that growing desire, in such a way as to lead men to see where the substance of true unity lies. But first, before we consider that, we must look *back*, and see how this new desire for unity has arisen. The first part of this lecture, therefore, will have to do with the relations of separated Christians with each other, as they have been, in the past, and with the beginnings of a far-reaching change of attitude, leading to what they will become, we believe, in the future. The second part of the lecture will deal with the eirenic dialogue between Christians proper to the new relationship between them which is coming into being.

We are standing, today, at the beginnings of a

great revolution in Christian history; an entirely unprecedented revolution. This revolution, the movement towards the unity of Christians, called the Ecumenical Movement, has already brought about, throughout the world, a tremendous change in the attitude of separated Christians to each other. What is the nature of this change of attitude? Whenever schisms have taken place in the history of the Church, we always find the same characteristics: they began by misunderstandings by some outstanding leader or leaders, who entered into controversy with other leaders on some question of revealed truth, and ultimately on the fundamental question of the divine authority which mediates that truth to men. This controversial warfare generated a kind of war psychology. War psychology, as we all know, puts insuperable barriers in the way of understanding between opponents. Enemies don't try to understand each other, or attempt to see from each other's point of view. They want to win a victory over each other. It's not a victory of love or reconciliation—it's a victory of power they want. They seek to force their opponent, by tactics of violence, in word or deed, to see from their own point of view, to acknowledge the rightness of their own position.

That is a characteristic of all warfare, from a private quarrel between individuals, to a world war between nations. In all such quarrels, as a rule, truth is probably involved. There is a right and a wrong somewhere, and it is seldom all on one side. But what obscures the truth, and prevents it being seen in its wholeness, is a hot cloud of hostility, which distorts and hides it, by false emphasis, and onesided propaganda.

In the great divergences between Christians, which have led to heresy and schism, the truth has always been *there*, because the Church has always been there; the Church founded by Christ and guided by the Holy Spirit; and the Church has always authoritatively defined the truth by dogmatic definition, which safeguards it from error. But in spite of this divine guidance, war psychology and its consequent distortions, on both sides, has too often made reconciliation impossible and has even at times led to heresy in the opposite direction. Amongst the great heresiarchs of history there may well have been a basic pride, that became the motive power of their revolt. Yet it is impossible to maintain that pride, and the hostility generated by pride, was all on the side of the heretics, and never disfigured the conduct of their orthodox opponents. Even in assessing the great heretics, their characters and motives, it is well to suspend human judgement, and leave the final verdict to God.

If, for instance, we compare the attitude of the leaders of the Nestorian heresy with the manoeuvres of St. Cyril of Alexandria against them, at the time of the Council of Ephesus, we are forced to see how disturbing to the intellectual and even the moral vision hostility can be, on either side. In the long-drawn-out history of the schism between East and West, from Photius to the Council of Florence, it is hard to judge which side bore the greater responsibility for causing misunderstanding and opposition; by the intransigent and controversial attitude it took up, by its failure to listen, and to elucidate what the other side was trying to say, and still more by motives for action which were far from the pure desire to get at the *real* truth underlying the problem in dispute.

Or take the deeply complex case of Martin Luther; the assessments of his three principal Catholic biographers in modern times vary considerably. The great Dominican historian, Denifle, makes him out little less than a rascal, whose later life was marked by a progressive moral deterioration; a generation later, Hartmann Grisar, his Jesuit biographer, shows him, and explains him, in terms of psychological maladjustment; yet in our own day, Dr. Lortz sees in him a prophet and reformer, who began with a deep Catholic insight into the nature of faith, but was diverted from his right course, and prevented from becoming the true reformer he should have been, at least in part, by the false picture of the Church presented to him by the considerable corruption of contemporary Catholicism.

Of course, these summings up of three biographies are generalizations, involving in each case a simplification of a complex treatment, yet they are true enough to teach us how warily we must approach the problems which lie at the heart of Christian disunity. And if this is true of the great protagonists in heresy and schism and their

orthodox opponents, how much more is it true
of us, their present-day descendants, the rank and
file of the multiple Churches of Christendom, in
our relations with each other. Hostility born of
war psychology, and issuing in partisan thinking
on both sides, has caused us to live for hundreds
of years in complete separation from, and rivalry
with each other.

This is true also of non-Catholic Christians
among themselves. We call ourselves separated
brethren, and we are so *technically* and in theory,
but the accent has usually been very much on the
*separated* and very little on the brethren. This
element of war psychology on both sides—orthodox and heretical—reaches back to the Church's
origins. The first heresy and schism was the rejection of Christ the Messias, which divided the old
Israel from the new. We see its development in the
Gospels and the Acts of the Apostles. It was not the
Chosen People who rejected Christ, but the pride
and blindness of their leaders. And ever since, the
history of Christianity has been bedevilled by the
war psychology *that* betrayal gave rise to.

"*The synagogue is not only a theatre*, it is a place of
prostitution; it is a den of thieves and of impure
beasts . . . The Jews live for their bellies, they
crave for the goods of this world. In shamelessness
and greed they surpass even pigs and goats; instead
of greeting them and addressing them with as
much as a word, *you should turn away from them as a
pest and a plague to the human race*." Those are not, as
we might suppose, the words of a Nazi leader in

Hitler's Germany. They were written by St. John Chrysostom. And, if the holiness of so great a saint and doctor of the Church did not cancel, on this point, the hostility of his war psychology and its resultant hatred, it is not surprising that this same war psychology has been shared down the centuries; among Christians, in regard to *Jews*, because theirs was the greatest of heresies, and by separated Christians in regard to each other.

We have all of us, in a greater or lesser degree, regarded each other from either side of the breach of schism, through the distorting spectacles of war psychology, and with the hostility that war psychology breeds. This is not, of course, to say that truth, and the fullness of truth, is not supremely important, or that error, wherever it appears, is not a very great evil, to be eliminated whenever possible by every legitimate means. But it is to say that error is never effectively eliminated by violence and hostility, but only by a love and friendship which is shown in a profound respect for sincere conscience, whatever errors such conscience may happen to approve, a profound respect, which extends to and recognizes also the *truth* that that sincere conscience also approves. Here lies the very groundwork of true charity, and the basis of the approach of separated Christians to each other, in their eirenic dialogue.

It is not an exaggeration, then, to say that this new eirenic attitude of separated Christians to one another, characteristic of the world-wide Ecumenical Movement, is a tremendous revolution,

which is only now at its beginnings. The origins of
the Ecumenical Movement lie, I believe, some way
back in history, in two other parallel and opposite
movements. The first of these was the great missionary expansion initiated by the Catholic Church
from Western Europe in the sixteenth and seventeenth centuries, and taken up also by the Protestant Churches in the late eighteenth and
nineteenth centuries. This movement reached its
climax in the twentieth century, when it became
virtually world-wide.

Side by side with this missionary movement has
developed a movement, also with its beginnings in
the Renaissance period, in the opposite direction.
The rise of humanism, in the fifteenth century,
developed during the seventeenth and eighteenth
centuries, by way of deism, and has now reached
its climax in our own day. We are today faced by a
humanism which, though it may sometimes retain
belief in God in some sense, denies all supernatural
revelation, and which in most of its manifestations
(and they are many), but notably in Marxist
Communism, seeks to eliminate the very idea of
God in human life altogether. The missionaries to
the heathen have found in the past, and find now
more than ever, that the great obstacle to the
spread of the Gospel, in pagan countries, is the
disunity of Christians themselves. Go back to your
own countries, the educated pagan tends in effect
to say, and settle among yourselves what the
teaching of your Christ is, and then perhaps we
will listen to you.

And the humanist, and above all the Communist, finds ample ammunition for his arguments and propaganda in the disagreements and inconsistencies of Christians themselves. The situation is the same, both among the rising nationalities of the transitional period, in the new worlds of Africa, Asia and the East, far and near—and also nearer home in the older countries of Europe and the Americas. We are faced by a grave world situation, in which over large areas of the inhabited globe, men and women are being taught that there is no God, that man is self-sufficing, and there is no need for God. Human life explains itself without him. And so the world is full of rivalry, hatred and the threat of war. This is the central crisis of our day—to this we have come.

We can hardly doubt that if Christians, through all the difficulties, doubts and struggles which mark the course of the Church's long history, had behaved more Christianly to each other, and to those who were not Christians—the world would now have been won for Christ to a far larger extent than it is. It may be, I think it probably is, that there are signs that all over the world there are men and women of good will looking for the means of reconciliation of man with man, in many fields of very different kinds. They can see already that violence, rivalry, cut-throat competition, and above all war, will destroy the world; and that men must live together in brotherhood or suffer that destruction. Perhaps we need, under God's providence, yet another world war of terrible dimensions, to teach Christians and non-Christians, all of us, that this ideal of brotherhood can only become a full reality under the rule of Christ.

This is the immediate reason for the urgent and rising call today, going out from the Christian world, for a united proclamation of the truth of Christ, the world's Redeemer and Lord; and this call is all the more urgent for us, because we know that the authentic voice of his Church is drowned, for the outsiders and the unbeliever, by a vast concourse of jangling and discordant voices, all claiming to speak in the name of Christ, and all saying different things about the means he has ordained for his message to be delivered to the world and his life of grace communicated to it and maintained in it. It is this that has made the Ecumenical Movement, in the course of fifty years, a world phenomenon.

It was Protestant in origin; it started from a missionary conference in Edinburgh in which Protestant missionaries from all over the world determined that if the world was to be won for Christ it must be by a wholly united message. The Gospel must not be divided. The Movement has grown, over the years since then, into a world phenomenon. To the great assembly of the World Council of Churches, its supreme organization, came last year to New Delhi, representatives of 175 Christian Churches from nearly fifty different countries. These representatives now include the Greek Orthodox, the Russian and other Eastern Orthodox Churches. The Catholic Church takes no part in official organizations sponsored by the World Council of Churches. In view of its unique claim (though this is shared, up to a point, by the Eastern Orthodox) to be the one true Church, it can hardly do so, at least in present circumstances, without danger of that claim coming to be looked upon as something the substance of which could be withdrawn or modified in the interests of unity.

But in the work of the Ecumenical Movement, particularly in its technique of encounter and dialogue between separated Christians, the Church is profoundly and deeply interested, and indeed involved, as is evident from this present conference. During the past two decades the Church has encouraged its theologians, in every country, to study the problems of ecclesiology from an ecumenical angle. Thirteen years ago came the first public gesture of interest on the part of the Church's supreme authority. In 1949 the Sacred Congregation of the Holy Office, under Pius XII, issued the Instruction to Local Ordinaries on the Ecumenical Movement (*Ecclesia Catholica*). That important document had little impact here in England and for a long time was not easily accessible in translation, though Fr. Leeming has now printed it in his book *The Churches and the Church*, and two years before that, in 1958, it was included in Bishop Bell's *Documents on Christian Unity*.

But the instruction contains very important principles, and is indeed a sort of charter of Catholic ecumenism. It attributes the movement

towards unity, among separated Christians, to the
work of the Holy Spirit, and it emphasizes that
reunion work *should daily assume a more significant
place within the Church's universal pastoral care*; with
this end in view it lays down safeguarding and
promoting regulations which would implement
this. Since then Pope John XXIII, with characteristic vigour, has taken many initiatives towards
Christian unity; the greatest of these being the
summoning of the coming Vatican Council, with
the purpose of facilitating a renewal of the inner
life of the Church, by reforms and adaptations,
which will enable its eternal and unchangeable
truth to be more clearly seen by, and therefore
made more attractive to, those beyond its borders.
The spearhead of unity work is of course the
Secretariat for fostering Christian unity, of which
His Eminence Cardinal Bea is President and
Mgr. J. G. M. Willebrands Secretary. All the work
of the Secretariat has been to promote contact and
encounter, friendship and exchange of knowledge,
between the Catholic Church and dissident
Christians, and this alone has already done much
to promote a friendly attitude between separated
Christians, which will foster the fruit that can
come from such encounter, and not least in for-
warding this has been the symbolic visit paid by
Lord Fisher, formerly Archbishop of Canterbury,
to Pope John XXIII. That visit has changed the
atmosphere astonishingly.

I propose now to turn to the second part of this
lecture, and examine the nature, aims, and some

of the difficulties, of the eirenic dialogue. Basic to all ecumenical work is the necessity of understanding, and in all human life understanding comes through love. It is the universal Christian precept to love one another. We have to make the effort to love, to be determined to succeed in the effort to love, all with whom we come into contact—even, as we know, our enemies and those who have ill-used or injured us. The basic principle of eirenic dialogue between separated Christians is to speak the truth in love. The differences are there, they divide us; we must never gloss them over or water them down. They must be entered into, and seen from each other's points of view—from the point of view, that is, of those who differ widely from us.

To undertake this is a difficult and *costing* work. It will be slow work, moving gradually, by way of a permeating influence, towards a cumulative result in the future. This result will not come about easily, or at once; we mustn't allow ourselves to think of this unity between Christians as being just round the corner. It quite certainly isn't. It will need tenacity and perseverance, and will have many setbacks. It may not be realized for generations, for centuries—we must be content with laying foundations. And whether it comes at all, will depend, on the human side, upon how far separated Christians, ourselves among them, are prepared not only to *give*, but to receive; to speak the truth in charity, to listen to what others have to say, and above all to listen to what the Holy

Spirit has to say to each of us through each other, especially through our humility, our integrity and our love of each other.

The non-Catholic cannot give us anything the Church does not possess, but our relation to him can help us to make that possession more deeply our own and so perhaps to pass it on to him. And even when all has been said and done, through friendship and understanding, that can be done, though much agreement may be reached, and many misconceptions cleared up, deep divergences may well remain. That is in God's hands; faith is a grace, God's gratuitous gift; and unity in faith—unity, that is, of belief in the authority that mediates faith—is the greatest gift of all. But if we are faithful in preparing the ground for the seed of this unity, then we may be sure that in God's good time he will make the seed grow and flourish till it embraces very many more of Christ's followers than it now does.

There are, I think, three principal obstacles in ecumenical encounter, obstacles which make such encounter difficult and are liable to cause it to fail. They are:

(1) Unconscious war-psychology, of which we have already said a good deal.

(2) A widely differing mentality and outlook between Catholics and non-Catholics, ultimately rooted in differing concepts of the nature of the Church's teaching authority.

(3) A great difference in our respective idioms of thought and language, in things religious.

We are like foreigners, speaking to each other in a language which each understands very imperfectly; on these three principal difficulties in the eirenic dialogue I will comment very briefly, with the object of stimulating fuller discussion of them in our group meetings. It is war psychology that lays heavy emphasis on the separateness of Christians and pays little or no attention to the fact that they are brethren. Yet we are *in fact* brethren in Christ; non-Catholics are often baptized sacramentally (or, if not, at least by desire) and because of this, they are united with Christ in his Church by grace, they are saved by being *at least in some sense in, or belonging to* the Church by grace; and that is a fact of far greater importance than the separation, lamentable as that is. The trouble about war psychology is that it is largely unconscious. Like all unconscious and latent fears, it stirs the emotions irrationally. A word, an expression from an opponent, jars on us and we begin to see red, and then emotion and not reason tends to take charge. And this tendency is increased by our widely differing mentality and outlook. Unconsciously, we expect non-Catholics to think like us, in our categories, we look for the same presuppositions in them as we take for granted in ourselves, and they simply are not there. They are not there because as Catholics we are

guided by the living voice of the Church's here-
and-now-magisterium, which touches our daily
lives at every point.

They have no such magisterium, and are
dependent for the interpretation of Scripture upon
digging into the historical past; their concept of
the Church involves seeing it as a divided entity,
and a divided Church can have no living voice
concerning its own nature and functions. Yet the
primary point of *our unity* is unity in Christ, and
we share that with non-Catholic Christians, who
can and do have true supernatural faith. The root
of *our disunity* is differing conceptions of the means
by which revealed truth is mediated by God to
men, and in consequence differing concepts of the
*content* of faith, the *extent* of our respective credenda.

The third obstacle to the eirenic dialogue—it is
the difference between separated Christians in
idiom of thought and language: Catholics are
the heirs of a long tradition of a scholastic
approach for the elucidation, in theology, of the
data of revelation. The scholastic theology of the
late Middle Ages was rejected by the Reformation—it was never a part of the tradition of the
Eastern Churches. There is therefore a twofold
gulf among separated Christians in regard to the
concepts and language of theology; that between
Eastern and Western, and that between Catholicism and the Reformation. It is no doubt true that
later scholasticism, in some of its manifestations,
both previous to and after the Reformation, tended
to be out of touch with the Scriptures, because it

used them as a quarry for proof texts, rather than what they are—God's word as a whole, treated as the primary source of the *res revelata*. It tended, therefore, to create the impression that the object of faith, and therefore of theological thinking, is a set of propositions about God, rather than the living God himself, speaking and acting in the person of his incarnate Son.

But this cannot be said of St. Thomas Aquinas, or indeed of any of the classical theology of Western Christendom at its best. This classical theology represented by the great scholastics is always a dynamic of theological thought for the elucidation of the living Word of God in Scripture. But the Reform, in separation from Western Catholicism, has developed during four hundred years a biblical theology of its own, independent of and out of sympathy with the scholastic approach. And scholastic theology itself, at the critical moment of separation, and indeed ever since, has sometimes shown, at least in some of its many manifestations, a tendency to substitute itself, at least in appearance, for the Word of God in Scripture. There is therefore a wide difference of language and approach between Catholicism and the Reformation; and this can only be resolved by an encounter, on a wide scale, in which each side is determined to listen to and understand the other, and in doing so to learn each other's language, and by doing so to realize, perhaps, that, at many points, both are largely saying the same thing, though in very different terms.

To some extent this is true of the relations
between Rome and the Eastern Church. What we
have been saying about differences of language
and idiom of thought between divided Christians,
makes the common study of the Scriptures, which
are our common possession as the Word of God,
one of the most necessary and fruitful starting
points for ecumenical dialogue. We have glanced
at the main obstacles to fruitful ecumenical encounter. How is this eirenic dialogue, so greatly
needed, to be implemented? The best means of
achieving it is by the organization of small groups,
on a wide scale, meeting regularly in round-table
conferences, tackling the central divergences
between us at the deepest possible theological
level. For this work priests will have to be prepared, or to prepare themselves by study. I take it
that this is the main reason for the calling together
of this conference by His Grace, Archbishop
Heenan, as the head of the episcopal committee
appointed by the Hierarchy for the promotion of
Christian unity. I should like therefore to suggest
six fundamental subjects for this eirenic dialogue,
subjects which go to the roots of the differences
that divide us from the rest of Christendom. There
are of course plenty of others, but these *six* seem
to me the most fundamental. I shall make a brief
comment on each, but only with a view to stimulating discussion in the discussion groups at a
later stage of the conference.

(1) *The nature of the biblical revelation and the nature
of biblical inspiration, together with its corollary of*

*inerrancy*. We are generally credited, except by a few non-Catholic scholars who know our biblical work on the Continent, with being complete *fundamentalists*, if not quite of the type who must believe that Mathusalah was actually and factually 969 years old, then something pretty near it. The new approach to the Scriptures, so much encouraged by the encyclical *Divino Afflante Spiritu*, can have a very great impact in showing non-Catholic scholars our freedom, our belief in sound scholarship, and the value of the guidance and protection of the Church's magisterium.

(2) *The nature of the faith which accepts the revealed Word of God*. Justification by faith alone, and our interpretations of its meaning (often very much of a text-book nature), was and is a cause of misunderstanding between Catholics and Protestants. Many years ago Cardinal Newman, as an Anglican, wrote his *Lectures on Justification* to show that between the Catholic and the Protestant view on this question there was a difference more of emphasis than of real divergence. His book was subsequently republished by him as a Catholic, with a preface in which he states that he still adheres to what he wrote as an Anglican. In our own day, the young German theologian Dr. Hans Küng has written a book (originally a Gregorian doctorate thesis) in which he shows the same thing, in regard to Karl Barth's teaching on justification and that of the Council of Trent. Barth remarks in a prefatory letter to this book that he is glad to find, if Küng's interpretation of Trent is correct,

that he is in agreement with the Church of Rome. There is a wide field for ecumenical dialogue here.

(3) *The relation of Scripture to Tradition*. There has been and is much diversity of view about this, as a book such as Fr. Tavard's *Holy Writ or Holy Church* shows, and the whole question is being widely canvassed, at the present day, in the theological schools. It would seem that the view that Scripture is *constitutive* of revelation, as being God's Word to men, and that Tradition, which is the Church's magisterium, is the *interpretative* element in revelation, is gaining ground. This would provide an acceptable avenue of approach for the discussion even of the extreme Protestant position of *sola scriptura*.

(4) *Theology, its nature and scope: reason and revelation*. The suspicion that permeates Protestantism, and to a lesser extent Anglicanism, as to the existence and validity of *natural law*, makes the discussion of this subject a necessity.

(5) *Development of doctrine: the "sensus fidelium" and the teaching magisterium*. The discussion of this has an intimate bearing on the truth and necessity of the *unicity* of the Church, as a divine society, visible and indivisible.

(6) *Infallibility, its nature and extent*. This also leads to the elucidation of the relation between the Papacy and the episcopate, in the teaching office of the Church; and so to the *unicity* of the Church's unity, the basic doctrine on which the Church's teaching authority is grounded. These topics must, I think, form the substance of the ecumenical

dialogue. The elucidation of each of them converges upon the central problem of unity and disunity, the nature and authority of the Church Christ founded. By way of conclusion I want to urge three practical points:

(1) The Instruction of the Holy Office (*Ecclesia Catholica*), the charter of Catholic ecumenism, we have called it, in providing for the promotion of reunion work as part of the Church's apostolate, says, that each diocese or group of dioceses should have offices and organizations to observe, examine, and direct ecumenical work as a whole and that suitable priests should be appointed to make a study of the ecumenical movement and everything connected with it. The extension of ecumenical work indicated by these provisions will in all probability involve some knowledge of, and sympathy with, ecumenical technique and ecumenical theology on the part of all priests. For a few, this will involve a fairly intensive study of non-Catholic sources (including some knowledge of the writings of Luther, Calvin and other Reformers) in connection with our own theology, and in addition considerable knowledge of much contemporary non-Catholic theology and other writings. For the majority, whose work would not admit of this, at least some acquaintance with ecumenical problems and the theology they involve would be necessary.

(2) The general growth of ecumenical friendship between Catholics and non-Catholics will inevitably lead (as it has already begun to do) to

eirenic dialogue among the educated laity at a
less than full theological level. The laity, as this
work grows, will need an increasing number of
priests, diocesan and religious, who are competent
to advise, instruct and safeguard the Church's
teaching in such dialogues, which have even now
begun and will inevitably grow, both as official
groups and in purely private conversations. How
can we priests be prepared for this, and seek to
exploit it on right lines? It is of course for the
Hierarchy to give directives, but we can help
these by our personal initiatives. I suggest that
reading and private study at least provide *some*
answer; to this end I have drawn up a bibliography of easily accessible books and articles in
reviews, which may be a help to priests to prepare
themselves for this work. I think the assessment of
these books and their scope and usefulness will
come up for discussion in our groups later on, so
I will not deal with this bibliography now.

(3) Finally, I need not remind you that prayer
is vitally necessary if reunion work is to be fruitful.
Not just occasional prayer, but constant prayer;
prayer by priests and nuns and lay people. And
perhaps above all, prayer together by non-
Catholics and Catholics, wherever and whenever
this is possible, without danger, and of course
under authority. In some ways I believe this is the
most important element of all; an element that
will break down unnecessary walls and build
bridges, where none now exist, which will lead to
true unity.

# 3. THE PRIEST: MINISTER OF UNITY

*Cardinal Bea, S.J.*

It was announced that this Conference would be in Latin, but I thought it would be easier to express these modern matters in a modern language, and I only hope that my English is not too offensive to your ears. It is a great joy for me to be able to address you today as priests who represent the secular and regular clergy of almost every diocese and congregation of the country— this country once so rightly called "The Island of Saints". Today, owing to events for which we do not wish to blame anyone, Christians of Britain are divided into many sects. This deplorable state of affairs reflects what prevails in the world at large, the division of the nine hundred million Christians scattered all over the world. Of these Christians, 32% of the world population, about 52%, a little less than five hundred millions, are Roman Catholics; 27·8%, or about two hundred and fifty million, belong to the communities originating from the Reformation; and 16·7%, equal to about a hundred and fifty million, are Orthodox or, in any case, separated Eastern Christians.[1]

To complete the picture, let us add that communities deriving from the Reformation are subdivided into more than two hundred groups. In the United States one can count two hundred and twenty-seven denominations officially recognized

by the State. The whole world, nevertheless, today
is tormented by a true longing for unity in its
public, social, and economic life. This is not only
on a national and international level, but on a
world-wide scale. The longing for unity among
Christians, moreover, becoming an ever stronger
desire, is all the more potent since it does not arise
from a merely human desire but from a divine
command. It goes back to the absolute will and
command of God and of the divine Founder of the
Church. It is, in addition, the action of a special
inspiration of the Holy Spirit, as it is expressed in
the well-known Instruction of the Holy Office
regarding the Ecumenical Movement.[2]

The unity of all who believe in Christ and who
have been baptized in his name is, one can say, at
the same time the strongest and the most profound
desire of the divine heart of our High Priest. The
priestly hearts of those who, by an infinite mystery
of grace and of mercy, share the character and the
mission of Christ the High Priest, must also have
the same ardent desire, must suffer from division
and long for the advancement of unity. We who
are gathered together here are certainly convinced
of it. This deep love for unity has gathered and
united us in this place. Therefore, in this spirit we
ask: How must the priest act to be in accord with
Christ's own idea and the will of the Church, in
order to become an authentic minister of unity
among Christians? How must he prepare himself?
What can he do to promote unity in the ministry
entrusted to him? How should he proceed?

## 1. General Preparation

If we speak here about the general preparation, it is simply a question of pointing out in more detail those elements of our priestly calling which bear a special relation to the work of unity. Having said this, it at once becomes evident that in a large measure, we have already made this general preparation. But since the Church's legislation obliges us to continue our formation, we might say that, in continuing it and in bringing it up to date, we must particularly bear in mind those elements that are most important in our apostolate for Christian unity. They can be collected under two headings: intellectual and religious formation, that is, personal holiness.

(1) *Intellectual Theological Formation.* The apostle of union must not only thoroughly know his own faith, so as to be able to move without danger amidst so many ideologies, religious systems, and the subtle reasonings among which he finds himself every day. He must also remain always up-to-date. By rethinking religious truths he must find solutions to those ancient problems which are always presenting themselves in new forms and under new aspects. Only in this way will he be able to move with security and find his way in the midst of so many new ideas. He will also be able to orientate others, by providing explanations, solving their problems and giving advice.

In this field philosophy is of particular importance, concerning both doctrine itself and the history of philosophy, that is, the growth of different systems of philosophy. We know, in fact, that several philosophical systems both express a particular mentality and, in turn, contribute towards moulding the mentality of men. It is inevitable, therefore, that philosophical systems have an influence on religious thought. This phenomenon affects our separated brethren all the more since their theology is not bound to tradition and does not remain under the control of a teaching authority. For this reason their language and mentality are largely dominated by the different modern philosophies. Only the priest familiar with the different philosophical currents will be able to understand and sympathize with them in their search for the truth.

Philosophy, however, only prepares the way to understanding. The proper field for the activity of the apostles of unity is the field of faith and of religious science, that is, of theology. It is here above all that the priest must excel with a wide and profound knowledge, so as to be able to give adequate answers and solutions to the problems which exercise the minds of our separated brethren. Neither should we delude ourselves by thinking that it might be enough simply to repeat the traditional proofs and the old distinctions. In the theological field—and here, perhaps, more than anywhere—there is a continuous tendency to evolve. The mentality of our separated brethren at the present time is not simply that of the sixteenth century, nor even of the nineteenth century. Our answers to their questions must therefore be relevant to the present situation. This presupposes further and continuous study and a deepening of our own theological knowledge. It is not a question merely of knowing the actual problems of our separated brethren. We must also have explored the possible points of contact. Those acquainted with the situation know how very useful and promising are the trends to be noticed in contemporary Protestant theology, which lend themselves to an extensive development. These can be of immense help to us and can help them more easily to grasp Catholic truth.

In a particular way, we must advance more and more in a solid and profound knowledge of Holy Scripture. While hundreds of millions of separated brethren base themselves exclusively on Holy Scripture, live spiritually by it and take it as the rule for their religious life, the priest coming in contact with them will not be able to understand them or convince them unless he be equally, or even more, imbued with biblical doctrine and a love for Holy Scripture. Continual reading of the Scriptures—of the Holy Gospels, of the Letters of St. Paul, of the Psalms, the Books of Wisdom and of the Prophets—and the deepening of the theological doctrine contained in the different passages and books—this, for the apostle of unity, is the indispensable preparation for his apostolate.

We must take note, moreover, of the spirit in which all this work has to be done. It is not a question of preparing ourselves for polemics. It is

rather a serene study inspired by a great love for
the truth, together with a great love for our
separated brethren. This twofold love will make
us discover many ecumenical aspects in those
problems where we probably never would have
suspected them. Where, according to the earlier
mentality, one could see only "adversaries", the
priestly view, guided by the love for unity and for
the separated brethren, will reveal to us brothers
in Christ, errant indeed, but still brothers. Them
we must love if we want to understand them and to
help them on the way to a full knowledge of the
truth of Christ and of his Church. I explained this
thought in an academic talk given last November
at the Catholic University of Fribourg in Switzerland, illustrating it by examples of philosophy, of
the history of dogma, of dogmatic theology, of
canon law and of Church history.[3] Afterwards
several professors expressed to me their joy and
also their regret at not having noticed such obvious
facts before.

(2) *Priestly Holiness.* Surely we do not need to
insist here on the necessity of holiness of life. We
know well that sanctity is not only the indispensable condition and the soul of the priestly
apostolate, but in its way—in so far as it depends
on us—it is its very source. The priestly apostolate
aims in fact at communicating—evidently in subordination to Christ and in co-operation with him
and the Church—the supernatural life of grace.
It is a general law that life can be communicated
only by those who possess it and that it can be

communicated only in the measure that it is possessed. The life thus communicated is as good as the life of him who communicates it. In the supernatural order of grace this means that the more one is intimately united to the source of grace, to the Holy Trinity, to Christ and to his Church, the mother of all the living, the better one can serve as an instrument in communicating grace.[4] Since unity is the work of grace, and even the work of grace *par excellence*, those who want to co-operate must possess the life of grace, and, therefore, sanctity, in an eminent degree. They will co-operate the better, therefore, the more they possess sanctity.

It will help to specify those special aspects of sanctity which are more necessary to, or which have more relation with, the apostolate of unity. They are all included in the word which indeed indicates the essence itself of all sanctity: "charity". First of all the love of God and of Christ which makes us embrace—with perfect identity of views in the Faith and in the unity of intellect and will— the whole doctrine, the whole truth of Christ which he teaches us through our holy mother the Church. The same charity moves us to do what we can to let our separated brethren partake in the fullness of truth and of grace. This charity will make our own the words of St. Paul: "The love of Christ spurs us on." (2 Cor. 5.14.)

We shall speak, later on, more specifically about the love of our neighbour. We want to stress here only one aspect which is of great importance for

the priest in his work for unity, namely, humility
and the high esteem and respect we should bear
towards our separated brethren. This springs from
charity, according to the words of St. Paul:
"Charity is patient, is kind: charity envieth not,
dealeth not perversely: is not puffed up." (1 Cor.
13.4.) Why are these virtues so important for the
unity apostolate? Because our separated brethren,
not being able to understand the exact meaning of
our affirmation that the Catholic Church is the
only true Church of Christ, reproach us with
being proud, with thirsting for power, a reproach
and a prejudice which has been strengthened by
centuries of controversial propaganda. In order to
obviate this obstacle there is—besides the prudent
and heedful explanation of doctrine—no better
means than the supreme effort of behaving more
than ever with a great Christian humility. We
shall, therefore, strive to hide behind the truth,
considering ourselves "useless servants" (Luke
17.10) of Christ. In our contacts with the separated
brethren we shall not seek anything other than the
truth. We shall not try to make them surrender by
force of argument but by force of truth. We shall
not seek to be triumphant ourselves, but look only
and always for the triumph of Christ and his truth.
Have not the saints always taken the greatest care
to accompany their preaching by an intense and
continuous exercise of humility? "God resists the
proud" (1 Pet. 5.5. James 4.6), says Holy
Scripture, and men do the same. We must imitate
the Holy Father who with great simplicity speaks

sincerely of his "humble person" and describes himself as "the humble successor of St. Peter".

To humility there must be joined the greatest respect towards our separated brethren, according to the saying of St. Paul: "Consider the others higher than yourselves." (Phil. 2.3.) This respect was warmly recommended to us in the general intention of the Apostleship of Prayer, approved by the Holy Father for the month of May of last year. This respect will also teach us the right way to propose the truth. Conviction in proposing it is proper, but this should not tempt us to despise the convictions of the brethren. These convictions have been inherited from their ancestors, deepened through their education, and are considered by them as a sacred trust. Of course, we may not, through a false eirenicism, abandon the doctrine of our holy faith or fall back into indifferentism, as if all confessions or religions were equally true. But neither may we despise those who belong to other confessions. Much less should we so insist in our arguments as to give the impression that we want at all costs to force others to give up their faith and to accept ours. Such methods do not take into consideration either the difference between the evidence and the objective certainty of a truth or the difficulty for man to understand and realize it. We must respect the secrets of the human heart and the freedom of man. Faith must necessarily be free: "One cannot believe unless one wishes to", says St. Augustine, and Pius XII, of holy memory, makes these grave words his own in the Encyclical

on the Church as the Mystical Body of Christ.[5]
If God, who is the absolute Master of man and
who investigates the most hidden mysteries,
respects the freedom of man and does not force
him, how much more should we poor creatures do
so in our relations with our own brothers!

## 2. THE SPECIFIC PREPARATION

Broaching the question of specific preparation,
we might start thinking at once of the study of
those confessions with which we mostly come into
contact. We must make a study of the Ecumenical
Movement, of the initiatives of both Protestants
and Catholics, in order to draw inspiration for our
own activity. All these approaches are necessary
and indispensable. That is why several competent
speakers will talk of them during this conference.
There are, nevertheless, aspects and questions
more fundamental. Many questions of principle
still enter in which are equally valid for all
ecumenical work, in whatever field it may be done.
I would like to lay stress upon this subject. To be
brief, it is a question of acquiring and enlarging
more and more in the light of our faith our vision
of the actual situation. We must see clearly the goal
to be reached, the persons involved, the obstacles
and the means. This vision has to be precise and
clear, realistic and balanced, but, above all, deeply
supernatural.

(1) First of all, a vision of the final goal, that is,
the unity we desire and which we have to attain.

(*a*) It is a question, above all, of a unity of faith, that is, the profession of the same faith by all who are baptized. Man today is surrounded by a real chaos of ideas, of philosophical and religious systems. It is easy to understand how today there can be a temptation to yield to a certain scepticism, to be ashamed of the intransigence of Catholic dogma as being narrow, hardly modern, little open to reality, something resembling fanaticism. A misunderstood love for the separated brethren could also lead to a certain levelling, to a false eirenicism. This would allege that, for reunion, all that is required is the recognition of those truths considered to be "essential", the fundamental dogmas, omitting all the rest or deferring all the rest to the future.

This, evidently, cannot be the way to true and authentic unity. There are surely among our separated brethren many elements of truth and piety, and we must recognize and acknowledge them with sincere joy. But, in spite of these good points, we may not ignore the differences and the deficiencies, particularly on essential points. The solid work for unity must first of all safeguard the integrity of Catholic dogma, constantly aiming at the sublime goal proposed by the Apostles: "Our common unity through faith, and fuller knowledge of the Son of God. So we shall reach perfect manhood, that maturity which is proportioned to the completed growth of Christ: we are no longer to be children . . . driven before the wind of each new doctrine that human subtlety, human skill in fabricating lies, may propound. We are to follow the truth in a spirit of charity, and so grow up, in everything, into a due proportion with Christ, who is our Head." (Eph. 4.13–15.) We must always keep intact this clear vision in all the works for unity, deepening it more, and having a fervent desire to share this precious treasure with all those with whom we have to deal.

(*b*) Besides the faith, Christian unity also is concerned with unity in the use of the means of grace which are the sacraments. There is already a certain unity in virtue of Baptism, as we shall see later on. A baptized person, whoever he may be, is not for us the same as a Moslem, a Buddhist, or a Brahmin. A baptized person is our brother in Christ, and we have to strive to let him share, not only the graces the Lord gives him in virtue of Baptism, but also all the other great graces which Jesus has placed in the hands of the Church, especially in the sacraments, above all in the august sacrifice of the Holy Mass and of Holy Communion. Now, these separated brethren do not recognize many of these sacraments as such. They thus deprive themselves of their salutary effects. In order to be an apostle of unity, the priest must first of all imbue himself with a great esteem and veneration of the holy sacraments and all the liturgical adornment that surrounds them. The liturgical movement, cultivated with unity in mind, is a precious help, all the more today, because the desire for a liturgical life is alive in the hearts of many of our separated brethren who are no longer satisfied with the sole ministry of the word of a preacher, in a place without any sacred character.

(c) Unity, however, would not yet be perfect without adding also the submission in matters of doctrine and of discipline under the Sacred Pastors, of apostles united among themselves, and with the supreme pastor, the successor of St. Peter, the Bishop of Rome. And this probably is the hardest among the requests we will have to make of our beloved separated Protestant brethren, who for many centuries have been taught that in the Church of Christ there is no authority that could bind the individual conscience of each of the faithful. The democratic idea which is today dominant in a great part of the free world, stresses and strengthens these sentiments of religious autonomy. The apostle of unity must therefore have a clear and concrete view of the hierarchical structure of the Church, founded by Christ, and of the great benefits coming from this hierarchical structure, willed by Christ. He will, above all, make it clear that this is certainly a question of the definite will of God, of the divine Founder of the Church, to which we have to submit ourselves. But, on the other hand, this mandate, and the hierarchical structure deriving from it, are sources of great graces. Through it the Hierarchy gives us directions in matters of doctrine and of religious practice. In fact, it is precisely this desire to have an authoritative guidance in religious life that has led and is still leading not a few non-Catholics to

the Catholic Church. The apostle of unity must
have an accurate idea of this prerogative of Christ's
Church and be acquainted with the blessings it
brings to souls.

(2) A clear idea is needed of the people with
whom we have to work, that is, the separated
brethren. I repeat that it is not a question here of
instructing one or other group of these brethren,
but of considering the separated brethren, whatever group they may belong to, from the stand-
point of our faith.

(a) The first aspect is the relation of these
brethren to Christ, to his mystical body and, therefore, to the Catholic Church.[6] Concerning this
relation the Catholic Church affirms resolutely the
general doctrine of the New Testament, that with
valid Baptism, even though conferred outside the
Roman Catholic Church, the baptized person is
organically united with Christ and his mystical
body. By grace he becomes the adopted child of
God, and, for this reason, all those who are validly
baptized are brothers. Now, since the Catholic
Church teaches that she is the true Church of
Christ, necessarily, she considers also those
baptized persons, who live separated from her,
as somehow belonging to her. They are "sons" of
the Church and our "brothers", and the Holy
Father calls these "separated brethren" also his
"sons". This he does not say and could never say
about those who are not baptized, who are not
Christian. It is true, of course, that these separated
brethren do not recognize the Catholic Church as

the true Church of Christ, consequently they are somehow separated from her and are not her sons and members in the full sense, as we Catholics are. They are separated from Catholics by differences in faith, in the use of the means of the life of grace, in the sacraments, and also by the fact that they do not recognize the authority of the Church and of the Roman Pontiff. These differences are certainly very serious, but still they do not destroy nor take away that certain fundamental belonging to Christ and to his mystical body and to the Church.[7]

From what we have said, the situation of our separated brethren regarding the salvation of their souls is clear. Having been baptized, and if in good faith they accept and live according to the faith in which they were born and have been educated, they receive, in virtue of their belonging to Christ, the necessary help for an authentic religious life, for the observance of the law of God and, therefore, for their salvation. They are thus on the way of salvation and this in virtue of that fundamental belonging to Christ and to the Church of which we have spoken. But of course, they are deprived of many graces and helps given by the Catholic Church to her faithful.

(b) The second aspect in the consideration of the separated brethren concerns *obstacles*.[8] Here, too, we must have a realistic vision, not deluding ourselves, but having the courage to admit facts. But, on the other hand, we must not allow ourselves to be drawn to pessimism or to exaggeration.

Truth is serious and does not need to be exaggerated. It is absolutely certain that on the way to union, mountains of obstacles still arise. All that heap of resentments, misunderstandings and prejudices, suspicions and mistrust, has accumulated through the centuries on both sides, and are more dangerous and harmful because often the persons concerned are not fully aware of them. We are often accused of pride, imperialism, and of claiming a monopoly of the truth. But let us come to the main and fundamental points, that is, to the *doctrine of the Church*, her nature and hierarchical constitution, the authority of the Church in matters of doctrine and discipline, by which she can really bind in conscience. On all these points there are divergencies more profound than ever, especially with regard to the communities originating with the Reformation, but partly also with regard to Oriental Christians in general and the Orthodox in particular. This is where the deepest chasm divides us.[9]

(c) But let us add at once the positive aspects as well, the flashes of light, though faint, that are starting to illuminate the horizon, and the small beginnings of approaching the Catholic doctrinal position regarding the threefold unity of the Church about which we have spoken above. In fact, more and more voices and appeals are heard asking for a clarification of the quality and the authority of the "ministers" of the Church and of their "ministry". There is a demand that this authority should have the opportunity and the courage to explain the doctrine of faith authoritatively enough to bind the consciences of its own faithful. They have begun, moreover, to affirm that, regarding Holy Scripture, it essentially belongs to and is committed to the Church and to her interpretation. It cannot, therefore, simply be interpreted by anyone according to a presumed or real inspiration, received from the Holy Spirit. Finally, on account of this trend, there is an increasing number of interpreters of Sacred Scripture, of learned theologians, who recognize that Jesus really conferred "the Primacy" upon Peter. They admit that he had the authority of the true Head of the College of the Apostles, though they contend that this primacy constituted only a personal privilege given to St. Peter and not a permanent institution which would pass on to the whole Church.[10]

Besides the flashes of light concerning doctrine, we must also underline the efforts made by our separated brethren, above all in the ecumenical field. This is a fact which we ought to understand and appreciate rightly—it is always the clear and balanced vision that matters! Right from the beginning we have emphasized the most painful state of division reigning among our separated brethren, especially among those springing from the Reformation. Let us underline now what with good reason can be called a gigantic effort to come, at least in some measure, nearer to that unity which is so eagerly desired.[11] I am speaking about "ecumenism", the "ecumenical movement" which at the present time is of so great an importance.

This movement originated outside the Catholic Church, but it started because of the desire of the separated brethren, divided in many groups, big and small, to find a way towards unity and towards a fraternal collaboration, especially in the missionary field. The movement tries to promote unity by means of international conferences, studies, scientific and theological research, reciprocal assistance and help, mutual endeavour to defend religious freedom, and in charitable and social activities. The most concrete expression of this movement is found today in the World Council of Churches, which includes 198 member-Churches, most of them Protestant of different denominations but with a certain number of Orthodox communities. Next to the World Council of Churches there is the International Missionary Council, founded forty years ago, and since last November "integrated" in the above-mentioned World Council of Churches. Catholic Christians can rejoice about all this for it is a powerful expression of the desire of unity. It is a phenomenon which fifty years ago was still impossible, and regarding which the well-known Holy Office Instruction on the Ecumenical Movement says that it is "the work of the Holy Spirit and the fruit of much prayer".[12]

We must realize that this unity is not yet the threefold unity described above, and which Christ has willed and implored from the Father. The Catholic Church cannot, as has often been asked and desired, become a member of this organization, which has a completely different character from the structure given by Christ himself to the Church he founded. But at the same time we must appreciate these achievements and pray that they may prosper more and more, and not stop in the middle of the way, in a purely practical unity. May they proceed courageously and help to prepare little by little that full and perfect unity willed by Christ.

### 3. MEANS OF ACTION

It is a question now of describing concretely what action the priest can take to foster Christian unity. Since we are speaking of priests in general, and not of those who may be specially appointed by their superiors, the question is this: what can the priest do for unity in the course of his ordinary priestly ministry? It is not a matter of deserting one's own duty, or of fulfilling it hastily and carelessly, in order to devote oneself to work for unity. It would be wrong to want to work for God in this way, disregarding his disposition of one's own daily life. What possibilities, then, does the ordinary priestly ministry offer for work for unity?

(1) The first and most important means is to preach untiringly the great duty of all the faithful to work for unity. We cannot say that the consciousness of this duty is very much alive among all Catholics, in every country. There is hope that the Council will awaken consciences also in this

regard. It is not necessary to repeat here at length
the reasons and the motives for this apostolate.
The fact is that our separated brethren, in virtue
of Baptism, already belong in some way to the
Church. But, at the same time, they are deprived
of many graces which would come to them if they
belonged fully to the visible organism of the
Church. The most elementary charity requires us
to do what we can to bring them to full membership of the Church. There is, moreover, the
absolute will of God and of the divine Founder of
the Church that all those who believe in him and
are baptized "may be one". There is, at the same
time, the importance of this unity for the world.
It is, in fact, seeing the unity of those who believe
in Jesus, that can lead the world to believe in Jesus,
that the "Father has sent him". (John 17.21.)
The world can find its salvation only in him.

Our century has received the immense grace of
three great movements that have entered deeply
into the consciousness of large strata of the faithful. There is, first of all, the consciousness of
the duty also on the part of the laity, to collaborate
in the apostolate of the Church. Hence the movement called the lay apostolate. There is likewise
the love for the Word of God, and for the Holy
Liturgy, in the biblical and the liturgical movement. There is, finally, the sense of responsibility,
incumbent on all Catholics, for the non-Christian
nations, and realized in the missionary movement.
Nowadays, a fourth movement has to rise, to assert
itself and to spread: the movement towards unity.

There is needed a sense of the serious responsibility of each Catholic for the brethren separated from us and for the reunion of all those who are baptized in Christ.

(2) The second means is to teach the faithful how to put this duty into practice and how to make practical a personal interest in all those who are baptized in Christ.

(*a*) The first and very first way to take an interest in unity is by prayer. The Sovereign Pontiffs, especially since the time of Leo XIII, have not ceased insisting upon the necessity of prayer for unity. A special occasion for this prayer is the Octave of Prayer for Christian Unity, which is observed now both by Catholics and by the separated brethren, from January 18th–25th. Not long ago our Holy Father John XXIII, in recommending the Octave, said: "With pleasure we make ours the words of our immediate predecessor of happy memory, expressing the pious wish that this practice may be spread in every region of the world, and, as widely as possible, especially in view of the Ecumenical Council." [13] For an individual, to attain to unity great graces are needed, to enlighten the mind, to strengthen the will, to overcome all the many obstacles. If these graces are already so great, as we know, for an individual conversion, how much greater must the graces be, in order that a group or whole community may find the way to reunion. Now this grace must be implored with humble, confident, persevering, and insistent prayer.

(*b*) In the second place comes the example of an authentic Christian life, to be given by all the faithful. This always makes a greater impression than words. The First Vatican Council said in one place that the Church is, according to the image used by the Prophet Isaiah, a sign lifted on high among the nations, which calls them to assemble.[14] The Holy Father John XXIII, in his turn, goes on repeating that the next Council should constitute—by the truth, the unity and love which will be reigning—a gentle invitation to the separated brethren to seek and rediscover that unity willed by Christ.[15] Both of these affirmations are also valid, in due proportion, for individual Catholics. They too should be in their surroundings a sign that points out the true Church and an invitation to join her. And this applies in a quite particular way in an environment where Catholics live every day with a majority of separated brethren, for whom they should be, by their exemplary Catholic life, apostles of unity.

We can perhaps insist once more on what the separated brethren expect particularly from us and what is the most efficacious means for promoting unity. It is that attitude of humility about which we spoke above. Our affirmation that the Catholic Church is the only true Church of Christ will be accepted much more easily if it is accompanied by the virtue which is the "innate" character of Christ's disciples: "Learn of me, for I am meek and humble of heart." (Matt. 11.29.)

Charity, a great love for all the separated

brethren we meet on our way—it is that charity which, although holding firm and unwaveringly to its own faith without compromise or division, at the same time is faithful to the warning of the Apostle of the Gentiles quoted above. (1 Cor. 13.4–7.)

Pope Pius XI once said to a group of Italian University students:

> The errors and the misunderstandings existing among the separated brethren of the East seem incredible, and they are constantly repeated against the Catholic Church. But Catholics also are sometimes lacking in a right appreciation of their separated brethren; sometimes fraternal benevolence is lacking, because knowledge is missing. One does not know all that is precious and good, and of a Christian nature, in those fragments of the ancient Catholic truth. Pieces broken off from auriferous rock are themselves gold-bearing as well. The venerated Christianities of the East preserve such a venerable sanctity of things that they are worthy not only of all respect, but also of all sympathy.[16]

We cannot say that these words refer only to Italy and to the relations between Catholics and Orientals. We must confess loyally and honestly that also in many other countries, and among Catholics and Protestants, there are on both sides many prejudices, many resentments and mistrust. All this can be overcome little by little, only by the effort to know each other and, above all, by a true and authentic charity.

(c) A last way to put into practice our interest in our separated brethren is the collaboration with them in fields where questions of faith do not directly enter in; especially in matters of social co-operation, of defending Christian principles in public, social and cultural life, in acts of charity, and especially in the relations among themselves.

This collaboration corresponds to the constant line of the teaching of Pope Pius XII and has been approved, since 1949, by the Congregation of the Holy Office,[17] and again inculcated by the Holy Father John XXIII, who makes a solemn appeal to all that "good-will placed at the disposal of order, justice, fraternity among all the Christian nations, contributing together in a common desire for comprehension, for deep respect in the three-fold order: religious, civil, and social".[18] To this order of things belongs also the great concern of the present moment, which is the preservation of world peace. What would it not mean for humanity, if the whole Christian world, nearly a billion men, nearly a third of humanity, would proceed completely united in the serious questions of, for example, nuclear arms, disarmament, peace!

After the enumeration of the means of priestly activity, let me emphasize once more briefly how important it is that all our activity be deeply supernatural. Today, a certain naturalism and activism continually lie in ambush, which too easily lead us to forget the importance of grace and the supernatural. This would deprive priestly action of its true content and, therefore, of its efficacy. Remember what we have said above: The more one possesses life himself, the more he can give it to others. The more he is united to the Blessed Trinity, to Christ, and to the Church, his bride, the more efficaciously will he be able to collaborate for unity. This holds for the priest himself as well as for all the faithful. Let us inculcate then, above all, the supernatural means that have the great advantage of being within the reach of each of the faithful.

## 4. Method of Procedure

We are referring here not to the way of proceeding in general—in this sense many of the things already treated, for example humility and charity, show the way of proceeding—but more specifically to the method to be adopted for action. It can be understood under three headings: Prudence, dependence on one's superiors, supernatural confidence.

(a) To be prudent and cautious. The work for unity can present some dangers even for him who is working for it. We have already noted that we should be well grounded in doctrine, constant and firm in our own faith and in its applications. It is all too easy to let oneself be caught by enthusiasm, even under the pretence of its being a question of a good and holy matter, and thus disregarding all

caution and measures of prudence. It is precisely
in holy things that much prudence is needed, for
Satan meddles quite easily with them, "trans-
forming himself into an angel of light" (2 Cor.
11.14), to reach his purposes, if for no other reason
than to spoil noble forces, to make one waste time
and compromise a good cause. Today, when the
nostalgia for unity is spreading more and more,
also among the strata of the faithful called "the
masses", we must also remember that mass
psychoses exist, fraught with illusions followed up
by most dangerous delusions. Such a dangerous
illusion, for instance, is the one noticed in several
polls of public opinion which have revealed that
many people expect from the Council the realiza-
tion of reunion itself.[19] That certainly is a utopia.
It is therefore much more important that the
priests, the spiritual guides, see clearly, that they
have a balanced vision, leaning neither towards
exaggerated optimism nor pessimism.

(b) The best guarantee, then, of not taking
the wrong way, is a close bond with the
Church's hierarchy, both with the diocesan
hierarchy of one's own bishop and the organs
appointed by him, and the universal one, the
Sovereign Pontiff and the Sacred Congregations.
It is this strong bond which preserves and protects
us from uncertainty, from risky and rash enterprises and from taking imprudent steps. The wise
directives of the Holy See, the fruit of rich experience, but above all given in virtue of that
assistance of the Holy Spirit promised to the

Church by our Lord, will help us to overcome all difficulties and to attain solid results for the salvation of souls and the welfare of Christ's Church.

Let us preserve here, too, a just balance. We are open, indeed, to the directives of the Holy See and to those that may come from the Council, but we shall fulfil them in subordination and under the guidance of our pastors. We must remember what we have already said above, that this dependence, besides being the will of God and a guarantee of the right path, is also a source of blessings and of graces for our activity. God leads us through the authority constituted by him, and he blesses obedience to it.

(c) Finally, we have need of a supernatural confidence, of "a faith that can move mountains". (Matt. 17.19.) The mountains exist, as we have seen. It is not a case of overstating the facts or of exaggerating. For this is clear: situations created over the centuries and reasserted from generation to generation cannot be changed in a short space of time, even with the most intense effort. We should have the courage to see very clearly the difficulties and the obstacles, but see also the work which the Holy Spirit is already doing. We should be patient, for with the Lord "a thousand years are like a day" (2 Pet. 3.8), but we must realize that the action of Christ and of the Holy Spirit, with whom we unite our weak forces, is irresistible. It is this thought which will give us an unshakable confidence and an invincible courage. Let us remember the words of St. Paul addressed to the

Corinthians, while speaking of his apostolic work:
"It was for me to plant the seed, for Apollo to
water it, but it was God who gave the increase."
(1 Cor. 3.) The result, the increase, is God's
concern. Prudence, dependence on one's superiors,
supernatural confidence: this is our great task,
which we must remember again and again ourselves and teach to the faithful. They too need this
very much in order to be able to proceed with
balance and according to the Spirit of God.

CONCLUSION

"God wills it": this is the decisive phrase in the
question of unity. We know that God wants it, not
only from the words of the Vicar of Christ and
from the other ecclesiastical superiors. God himself
is manifesting it through many circumstances,
which during these last decades have come together so wonderfully towards the great goal of
unity. Twelve years ago the Holy Office, in its
Instruction on the Ecumenical Movement (20 Dec.
1949), was able to write: "In many parts of the
world . . . under the inspiration of the Holy
Spirit . . . a desire has awakened and is growing
daily in the hearts of many, who are separated
from the Catholic Church, that unity may be
accomplished among all who believe in Christ the
Lord." [20] This is still more true today. It is proved
by the wonderful reactions of non-Catholic
Christians to the announcement of the Council,
reactions which are always improving, while

twenty years ago they would still have been in-conceivable.

It would be a great pity not to wish to hear this strong voice of circumstances, wisely guided by God's infinite and fatherly providence. Christ himself, a few hours before his passion and death, implored from his Father the everlasting unity of his Church: "I pray for those who are to find the faith in me, that they may all be one . . . as thou, Father, art in me, and I in thee", and he added a reason particularly memorable: " . . . so that the world may come to believe that it is thou who hast sent me". (John 17.20–21.) The heart of the priest must beat in perfect harmony with the heart of our High Priest.

The unity of all those who believe in Christ must also be a testimony to Jesus' divine mission. How necessary is this testimony today for the world! A great part abandons more and more not only Christianity, but God himself, professing a formal atheism. Many sections of humanity, meanwhile, are tempted with diabolical methods and systems to forsake faith and all religion. To oppose this un-believing world, it is necessary to present a world united in Christ and with Christ in the "una, sancta catholica et apostolica Ecclesia". To reach this sublime goal all Catholics, and first of all we priests, must confidently collaborate. Let us offer ourselves, therefore, to this noble work, in order that we may give our contribution to the realiza-tion of the desire of Christ: "Ut sit unum ovile et unus pastor." (John 10.16.)

NOTES

[1] The various sources of statistics differ considerably. We have chosen to follow the more balanced estimates. One may consult *Bilan du monde*, Paris and Tournai (1, 1958–9, 2, 1960) 1, 119–22, 140–42, 175–81; *Atlantino Missioni* (Venice, 1960) p. 25; K. L. Franklin and H. H. Walz, *Weltkirchenlexikon, Handbuch der Ökumene*, Stuttgart, 1960 (on the end-papers).

[2] Cf. *Act. Ap. Sed.*, 42 (1950), p. 142.

[3] Cf. A. Bea, *Akademische Forschungs- und Lehrtätigkeit im Dienste der Einheit der Christen* (Freib. Universitätsreden, new series, 24, Freiburg (Switzerland), 1962, pp. 9 ff. (The same article in French in *Nouv. Rev. Théol.*, 94 (1962), pp. 115 ff.)

[4] Cf. A. Bea, "San Paolo sull' essenza e l'importanza della vita interiore", in *A. L. A.* (*Rivista delle religiose d' Italia*) nos. 9–10, Sept.–Oct. 1961, pp. 8 ff.

[5] Cf. *Act. Ap. Sed.*, 35 (1943), p. 243.

[6] For a longer exposition of this question consult A. Bea, "Il Cattolico di fronte al problema dell' unione dei cristiani", *Civ. Catt.* (1961), 1, 113–29; especially 122–6.

[7] We are of course supposing the good faith of our separated brethren. Cf. "Il Cattolico di fronte al problema dell' unione dei cristiani", p. 121.

[8] The subject has been treated more extensively in my article, "Ostacoli all' unione dei cristiani", *Messaggero S. Cuore*, Rome, Dec. 1960, pp. 577–86.

[9] For more particulars cf. A. Bea, "Il Concilio sulla via dei protestanti", *Civ Catt.* (1961), 3, pp. 561–72; 4, pp. 3–13.

[10] For some examples cf. A. Bea, "Die Bedeutung des 2. Vatikanischem Konzils fur die Einheit der Christen", *Stimmen der Zeit*, vol. 170, no. 87 (1962), pp. 241–58, esp. pp. 250 ff.

[11] See for example J. P. Michael, *Die Christen suchen eine Kirche*, Freiburg im Breisgau, 1959 (the same work appeared in Italian with a good bibliography, Brescia, 1961).

[12] *Act. Ap. Sed.*, 42 (1950), p. 142.

[13] A letter to the Superior General of the Franciscans of the Atonement (October 28th, 1959) in *Acta et Documenta*

*Concilio Oecumenico Vaticano II apparando*, ser I, vol I, Città del Vaticano, 1960, p. 54f.

[14] Cf. Denzinger, *Enchir. Symb.*, no. 1794.

[15] Cf. *Acta et Docum.* (l.c.) I-1, p. 15.

[16] Address of 8 Jan. 1927, cit. D. Bertetto, *Discorsi di Pio XI*, Turin, 1959, 1, p. 671.

[17] Cf. *Act. Ap. Sed.*, 42 (1950), p. 145.

[18] Christmas Broadcast 1958, cf. *Act. Ap. Sed.*, 51 (1959), pp. 10f.

[19] One inquiry was made by the Bavarian Catholic Action, another in France; cf. A. Bea, "Die Bedeutung" etc., p. 241; *La Docum. Cath.*, 15 April 1962, vol. 59, pp. 502 ff.

[20] Cf. *Act. Ap. Sed.*, 42 (1950), p. 142.

## 4. ENGLISH CATHOLICISM AND THE ANGLICAN TRADITION

*Gordon Wheeler*

THE terms of reference in this paper are our ecumenical relations with the clergy of the Church of England. Clearly these may be divided into two groups: those who come to us for instruction and reception and those others to whom we should be going out, in the spirit of Pope John XXIII, for a greater mutual understanding. We shall thus be dealing in turn with two quite different techniques. The paper is called "English Catholicism and Anglican Tradition", because in the course of it we shall be examining two very different cultures which have, nevertheless, derived from a common root. The approach will be psychological and historical rather than dogmatic and I hope you will forgive some personal reactions which I dare to hope will make for practical suggestions; you will not agree with them all; but at any rate I shall have stimulated discussion and, as Cardinal Gasquet unsuitably said to Pope Benedict XV, "None of us is infallible."

We all probably know from our own experience how vitally important it is in helping converts into the Church to show the greatest possible understanding, sympathy and kindness. And if this is true of any conversion work how much more important is it in the case of a clergyman who is not only passing through an acute mental and spiritual experience but is also faced with the violent disruption of a vocational career and the usual consequent economic dilemma. Again, if this is true of the bachelor—and I know from my own experience twenty-six years ago what agonies such a person endures with the family tensions— indeed there is nothing so hard in life as to have to hurt those one loves most—the temporary loss of friends and the uncertainty about the future, how infinitely worse it is for the married clergyman, whose wife probably cannot understand what he is doing and whose family is about to be shipwrecked and to be deprived of all its security. The wife, in a sense, is called to make the biggest sacrifice of all because however much the man finds his feet in a new professional sphere the woman can never again achieve the unique position of status which this country accords the clergyman's wife.

When the convert clergyman comes our way it will be for us to judge what stage he has reached. He may be ripe for reception or he may be quite unready for months or years. It will not take us long to discover exactly where he stands. In these preliminary talks we shall frequently have to advise him to wait and study and pray longer. I myself was convinced intellectually four years before my reception. Many of my friends and acquaintances, cleverer and better than myself, were in the same position and did nothing about it. Why should I? This is difficult for the cradle

Catholic to understand. It looks as though there is
bad faith. Objectively, there probably is, but not
*subjectively*. Anglican habits of thought are radically
different from ours and the Englishman distrusts
the easy syllogisms and prides himself on his
illogicality. This is to a high degree inculpable and
derives from that comprehensiveness and ambiguity so distinctive historically of the Anglican
development. One thing is certain; the vital
importance always to assume the subjective good
faith of these people. Ripeness for reception has
usually only happened over a long and agonizing
experience mentally, spiritually and consequently
even physically.

The test of the ripeness is to my mind clear and
simple. There comes a day and an hour when the
clergyman knows that no matter what the cost he
cannot function in his office (and especially in
saying the Communion Service) again. When he
has reached this stage he is ripe and must move.
Some of our Continental brethren who have no
experience of this important psychological factor,
have tried at this stage still to deter him in the
interest of a possible ultimate corporate unity.
They cannot know what they are doing because
there could not be a clearer example of thus
making the end justify the means. From this
moment he *must* go forward and become a Catholic
whatever the cost, and he knows it. He would be
subjectively and objectively in bad faith if he
remained any longer where he was. I have stressed
the importance of this because I have known great

distress and conflict arise from hearing such advice.

When the would-be convert clergy come our way they need every ounce of compassion we can give. Sympathy alone is not enough. At this stage they can no longer think or act for themselves and our assistance must be practical and self-sacrificing. The occasion demands and assuredly warrants great generosity of time and inexhaustible patience. If we meet it in this way it will have fruitful repercussions for the individual concerned but also more far-reaching consequences as his friends learn how he has been treated. I have always found it helpful to these people to point out that becoming a Catholic is not a denial but a fulfilment. It is true they are called upon to abjure heresy and schism. But I have never known one who had any difficulty about this. They are much more worried about a frequent misapprehension that they have to deny past graces. It is a comfort for them to be told that God is not circumscribed in this matter and that they have doubtless received many actual graces.

First, regarding actual instruction and reception into the Church. Remember that, unlike most other converts, he has already burned his boats. In addition, he knows by virtue of his training and study all the principal tenets of the Faith. I am not pretending for a moment that he knows enough to be ordained right away as a Catholic priest. His course and the terminology in which he thinks are entirely different from the

seminary training. It will take him years to think
as a Catholic. But generally speaking, he has quite
sufficient knowledge to be received *quam primum*.
Individual cases of course vary, but it would be a
splendid national gesture if our bishops would
instruct their curias to grant the faculty at once
on the judgement of the priest who is handling the
case. My own ordinaries have been most helpful
in this matter and the late Cardinal Griffin gave
me permission to send such people for a week or
fortnight of retreat in a monastery in which they
had the opportunity daily of conversing with a
priest, and were afterwards at once received. They
were thus given an admirable opportunity of
private and fuller instruction, especially on the
doctrine of the Church and Papacy and matters
like indulgences, which can always do with fuller
clarification.

I should like here to say that statistically there
is no warrant at all for the notion in some quarters
that those who do not go through long periods of
instruction subsequently apostatize. I am certain
that once you are sure of your man you should not
keep him waiting. The "no-man's land" is an
agonizing desert. I should like to see this gesture
recognized for the whole country. What about
conditional baptism? Most convert clergy expect
this after it has been fully explained to them.
I should think that most Anglican baptisms are
validly administered nowadays both as to matter
and form. It was not always so. Many royal
baptisms in the eighteenth and nineteenth

centuries were invalid because the Archbishop of Canterbury said the words whilst the Archbishop of York poured the water. Sometimes no water was poured at all. I know of one convert clergyman who produced a tape-recording to attempt to prove the validity of his son's baptism. And I know there are some priests who think that after careful enquiry Anglican baptisms should be accepted, and that there should be no recourse to conditional baptism. Perhaps they are right. Generally speaking, however, I find that most converts feel that they have been wallowing in doubt and uncertainty all their lives and now they want to be sure about everything. It is also a most helpful gesture if the bishop (as often happens with us) is so kind as to confirm the convert privately in his own oratory. This is a welcoming gesture of real significance.

We must be practical about the spiritual things and also practical about the material ones. All priests who meet with these cases should be in touch at once with the Converts' Aid Society, established at the request of Pope Leo XIII, and which has been pontifically and suitably described as "this most exquisite charity". This society is providentially well supported and does far more than most people realize to smooth the path materially. Clearly it can do nothing until after reception. But then it is extraordinarily zealous and not only deals with immediate material problems, but also undertakes the training of suitable convert clergy for other professions; sees to the maintenance of wives and families, buys suitable houses in which the *neo-conversi* may live in areas near to their newly-found work as school-masters, lawyers, etc. In addition it runs G. K. Chesterton's old house, Top Meadow, Beaconsfield, as a transit house for those who have had to vacate the vicarages and have not yet had time or means to settle elsewhere. This is one of the great welcomes which the Church gives to convert clergy and of course it has a special value for the married ones.

The bachelor convert clergyman often wants to go on to the priesthood. And here the Church makes her second welcoming gesture: the Beda College, Rome, created in its present form precisely for this purpose. Six or seven years of an ordinary seminary seem an endless eternity to the convert clergyman who, generally speaking, has already completed a university as well as a theological course. Surely part of the purpose of the longer duration is the testing of vocation on other scores. This is generally unnecessary in the same degree for an older man, who is more sure of himself and who has intellectually reached a maturity in which he can cover the ground of study more speedily. *Christo Spectante Curramus* is the Beda motto. The course is a complete one and all the usual tractates in Latin are covered. The generosity of the Holy See in creating the Beda is surely a model of wisdom and charity to be followed. Most of our bishops seem happy to send convert clergy-men there and many products of this unique seminary are playing their full part in the pastoral life of the country. Sometimes the bishop will advise the convert clergyman to remain for a year or two in ordinary life as a Catholic layman. This is sometimes wise and rightly decided according to the individual concerned. I myself was anxious to waste no time, and Cardinal Hinsley kindly arranged for me to be at the Beda within three weeks of my reception. It was a great relief to be in the heart of Christendom and away from all acrimonious controversy.

The important thing for all of us is to *present* the convert clergyman who is anxious to go on to the priesthood to a bishop. Otherwise he just does not know how to set about it. The whole idea of vocation has a new and different significance and he seldom realizes this at first. Outside the Church a "vocation" is almost invariably entirely subjective in concept. The prospective parson chooses his own university and theological college and the bishop in whose diocese he is offered an appointment ordains him. He serves for a year as a deacon and then is normally ordained completely by the same bishop. After two years he can move to any other appointment in any other diocese in the Anglican world. All the choices are his own. He looks down the columns of the *Church Times* for suitable vacancies and then wonders if he has gone to the right place. The Catholic subjection to authority in this matter is something which the convert greatly welcomes. *He knows* he is in the right place, and the assurance counteracts many difficulties. But it is an idea that has to be absorbed and which is against the whole of his tradition.

We must not be impatient with him if at first he appears to throw his weight about. I find it very important always to give the convert clergyman who would be ordained some idea of this radical difference. When he sees it clearly, as he must, he will at once submit to the will of the bishop regarding both the seminary chosen for him and all his subsequent appointments. I think it is important that he should not ask to go to the Beda. On the other hand, it is puzzling both to me and to him when he is not sent there. After all, it was papally created for this purpose. As to the choice of diocese, I think there is something to be said for directing the older man to a country diocese where he may have the opportunity of becoming a parish priest before he dies. He should have our help, our interest and our encouragement all the way through.

The problem of the bachelor who goes on to the priesthood is relatively easy. Much more difficult is the lot of the married man. Very often he is equipped for nothing else but to be a clergyman. And he usually has a strongly developed pastoral instinct. Sometimes he has sufficient qualifications to become a teacher and get on the Burnham Scale. This is the most popular solution, because it has clear apostolic aspects. But it is not always possible, either because of qualifications or from the temperamental viewpoint. Others go into banks, industry, the law; I know one who is in the finance department of a diocesan curia. Others are doing market-gardening and I have even found one washing up dishes in a restaurant. This is a pathetic state of affairs and a great challenge surely to us. We need machinery to help them more satisfactorily into the right milieu. We must do all we can to help each individual case and pull all the strings we can for them. It is small wonder that so few come in—ten to twenty per annum—when the right niche is not even found for this small number. The recently formed Blessed Cuthbert Mayne Society is trying to do something to help in this matter.

I pray myself that one day the Church may make yet another gesture to help these splendid men who have literally left everything for the Faith. I would not myself go so far as to ask for the dispensation from celibacy for the priesthood. The economic difficulties would be incalculable and many other difficult problems, such as integration, would arise as well. Besides, it is our experience that our people have a high regard for the celibate priesthood. I would, however, like to see a married diaconate wherein these men could exercise a useful pastorate in addition, perhaps, to doing an ordinary job. It is the pastorate which they miss and they could find fulfilment—many have told me so—in instructing, visiting, giving Holy Communion from the tabernacle in country places where the priest is perhaps only available once a week, and in general establishing the life of the Church in outlandish places. This is still in many

ways a missionary country—especially away from
the great towns—and a new impact could be
made by the zeal of such men. This present
pastoral frustration which can rarely find a full
outlet in the lay apostolate is something that ought
to be remedied. They would willingly go through
the necessary training.

What other difficulties does the convert encounter when he becomes a Catholic? Most that
I know would tell you that they have found
fulfilment in the Catholic Church and that they
thank God every day of their lives for what
happened to them.

At the same time there are certain things they
miss: unessentials it is true, but connected with the
specific Anglican culture. Curiously enough,
I think they all come under the heading of
liturgy in its broadest sense. Anglicanism, in its
own way, is highly liturgical. The smallest parish
church, as well as the great cathedrals—both inherited from Catholic days—have splendid volun-
tary choirs and full participation of the people in
all worship. The services of Morning Prayer and
Evening Prayer, constructed on traditional lines
and taken largely from the projected breviary
reform of Cardinal Quiñones in the sixteenth
century, with Venite, psalms, Benedictus, Te
Deum, Magnificat and Nunc Dimittis, with
scriptural readings and venerable Collects, and
the Communion Service with many characteristics
of the Mass, all these are fully rendered everywhere
with dignity and beauty. Moreover, there is a

tradition of hymnology which for the ordinary Englishman is an integral part of his religion. This is in no sense a plea for the vernacular. On the contrary, the traditional forms of Anglican worship have become so archaic as to be no longer vernacular; and the Archbishops of Canterbury and of York are now asking for Parliamentary legislation to enable them to experiment with other forms. By and large, however, the Book of Common Prayer is still "understanded by the people".

The more progress made by the liturgical reforms and directives of Pope Pius XII and Pope John XXIII and the more participation in the Mass penetrates our churches, the more the converts will feel at home and other non-Catholics be drawn to the Faith. The further, therefore, we can implement the decrees *De Musica Sacra*, and promote the mind of the Church regarding the dignity, beauty and participation in worship, the more we shall be remedying this particular problem. We have the great witness in this respect of our abbeys and other religious houses and some of our cathedrals and churches. We must infiltrate, however, this tradition to the smallest outposts. The English are a liturgical people and we can do much to win them by the Liturgy, which in its proper forms far surpasses anything they possess. They also miss being used by the priests in the way they made use of the good layman. Here the development of the lay apostolate has an important part to play. With regard to this in the Liturgy we are in a strong position. Let us make full use of it for the glory of God and the conversion of souls.

The biographies and writings of Cardinal Wiseman and Cardinal Manning—and to a lesser degree of Cardinal Newman, who was more cautious—suggest that these great men would have been disappointed by the twentieth-century rate of conversions. The considerable growth of the Catholic Church in England has indeed been largely due to the new waves of immigration and the "second spring" has never really become a summer. There has been in fact no considerable impingement on the Anglican fortress. Even if Pope John XXIII had not urged us to approach the whole question in a new way we should have done well to accept the fact that ten to twenty clergymen and ten to fifteen thousand of the laity *per annum* made very little difference in millions and when we were losing many also by lapsation. Now, thank God (and who is there to say it is not providential?), we approach the whole problem in a new way. And whilst the individual conversions can and must continue, we are in a new-found dialogue with Anglicanism as such. No longer are our contacts confined to those on the brink. We are in a close relationship with those whom we repel rather than attract and with whom the greatest common link (apart from the "vestigia verae ecclesiae", Scripture, Baptism and a great veneration for the past) is the prayer and yearning on both sides "ut unum sint".

Perhaps you may consider this a sweeping

generalization. I do not think so. I know there is a
tiny group in the Anglican Church which holds all
the teaching of the Catholic Church and accepts
the infallibility of the Pope, jibbing only at the
constitution *Apostolicae Curae* of 1896, which declared Anglican orders invalid. All I want to stress
for the moment is that this body is totally un-
representative of Anglicanism and even of Anglo-
Catholicism as such.

The Anglican Bishop Wand in his magnificent
volume *Anglicanism in History and Today* (1962),
himself belonging to the large Anglo-Catholic, as
against the small Anglo-Papalist party, was content to define Anglicanism in the words of the
*Oxford Dictionary of the Christian Church* as follows:
"The system of doctrine and practice upheld by
those Christians who are in religious communion
with the See of Canterbury; it is especially used,
in a somewhat more restricted sense, of that system
in so far as it emphasizes its claims to possess a
religious outlook distinguishable from that of other
Christian communions *both Catholic and Protestant*."
(I find that a great many Catholics think "Anglicanism" applies only to the High-Church members of the Church of England. This is of course
untrue. It comprehends *all* parties and is a generic
term.)

Later on in the book he delineates four traits
that seem most characteristic of the Anglican
ethos: comprehensiveness, belief in continuity,
emphasis on the Bible, and a clinging to national-
ity. I think myself that this is about as fair an

assessment of Anglicanism in general as you will get anywhere; and indeed the book might safely be used as a basis for ecumenical discussions with any mixed Anglican group. It is important never to forget or underestimate the highly Christocentric Anglican piety which has its own literature and transcends all divisions and parties.

Dr. Wand has in this book an illuminating section on the development and evolution of the historic parties in the Church of England: the High and Low Church, the Broad Church, the Latitudinarians, the Evangelicals, the Anglo-Catholics, the liberals. We shall constantly be confronted with the widely differing beliefs, all comprehended in the Church of England, which are the legacy of the ambiguities of its formularies. Most Anglicans would now admit that the Thirty-Nine Articles are the greatest masterpiece of ambiguity of all time. The first four General Councils provide a much better jumping-off ground. With Anglicanism let us never delude ourselves that we have got the whole picture. The only thing they really have in common is a great personal love of our Lord, even when they are not quite sure who he is.

What then must be our approach to the Anglicans? The mandate which the Holy Father gives us is to be found in Ephesians 4.15: "Veritatem autem facientes in caritate, crescamus in illo per omnia, qui est caput Christus." A programme of truth and charity, the two indissolubly united. For, as Your Eminence has truly said, "Truth without charity becomes intolerant and destroys charity. Charity without truth is blind and passes away."

Our new approach to Anglicanism, as such, calls for a different technique from that employed regarding individual converts. The end in view is ultimately the same: the triple unity which Your Eminence delineated. The Catholic Church is at all times essentially the "spotless bride of Christ". Accidentally, however, she can be enriched and in a sense it can be said that different groups and different nations can contribute to this enrichment. The late Fr. Bede Jarrett used to say with characteristic humility that the Dominican Order could contribute much to the life of Oxford, but that Oxford could also give something to the Dominican Order. Would it be rash to say that there is a sense in which the particular Anglican genius or stress has an accidental contribution to make to Catholicism? Our possible acceptance of this idea could greatly facilitate our dialogue with Anglicanism and give it an additional purpose. We should then approach Anglicans not only with that crediting with good faith which is so important, but with a realistic humility in which we should be prepared to share and appreciate some of the gifts which they have to bring. This climate can make true dialogue possible. Our policy, anyhow, will be a long-term one. Here we shall not be aiming at individual conversion (though we must never circumscribe the action of the Holy Ghost in any individual). We shall be speaking the truth in charity, acknowledging our own faults

and drawbacks, being ready, in humility, to learn,
and *leaving the rest to God*. Do not let us look for
startling results. Meeting together and studying
together with great patience and understanding
is all that matters for the moment. Here we shall
be following the papal directions and by our un-
questioning obedience God will, in his own time,
bring about results far surpassing our imagination.

This meeting and studying should be taking
place on different levels; the outstanding scholars
on both sides; but similarly, under episcopal
guidance, on other planes. The spirit of ordinary
friendliness engendered can do much.

The truth, we know, is unalterable fundamentally. There is constant room, however, for
clarification and explanation in the knowledge and
language of our times. This is true both in
philosophy and theology and, especially, of Scripture. Here I would like to point out in passing the
inestimable benefits that would accrue from a
commonly recognized English version of the
Scriptures. I should like to express the hope that
our Hierarchy may soon consider this possibility.
I believe I am right in saying that something like
the Revised Standard Version could well be sanc-
tioned on our side in the way that has been done
by our friends in the Anglican and Free Churches.
Already publishers have indicated a solution to
what our separated brethren call "The Apo-
crypha". The Anglican Church has a special love
for the Scriptures and a lectionary of daily reading
far wider and more all-embracing than our present

breviary lessons. This knowledge and evaluation of Scripture is not only something we should emulate but provides, perhaps, the best possible opportunity for mutual agreement and enrichment. Father Henry St. John has given us a splendid programme in this respect.

I would add that the nature of the Church is also a most fruitful field. This is true nowadays, I believe, with regard to all our separated brethren. But if it is true of Lutheranism and Presbyterianism, how much more so with regard to Anglicanism, which has maintained at great cost (e.g. "the martyrdom of Charles I") the Church's traditional and monarchical episcopate. If she appears to have sacrificed this principle as a temporary measure to further unity (wrongfully, as many will admit who hold with us that the end does not justify the means), I think we can be quite sure that it will never be lost. From this it is not an insuperable task, generally speaking, to get Anglicans to accept the Primacy of St. Peter and his successors. They regard it, however, as one of honour or, better still, of service ("Servus Servorum Dei"), than of infallibility. I have heard them deplore the scandal of not being in communion with Peter. Again, they regard the Church in the scriptural terminology of the Acts, and here surely we have a great common legacy. Two of the distinctive traits of English Catholicism for the first thousand years of its history were a great veneration for the Papacy and a great love of our Lady, which caused this country, so rich in

shrines, to be called the Dowry of Mary. I think
it is evident that these characteristics have been
maintained through the days of persecution and
are present in English Catholicism today. I think
also that English people receive these doctrines,
when they are elucidated theologically, in modern
terminology, with surprisingly little opposition.
The patristic approach to the Church as the Bride
of Christ, drawn from his side on the Cross, as
Eve was from Adam, gives them at once the concept of a living body. Similarly, I have never had
any difficulty in at any rate opening their eyes to
the reasonableness of the Assumption when I have
explained it in terms of "the resurrection of the
flesh", which they recite in their Creed as we do, and
the suitability of its anticipation for the Mother
of God. They are much more unhappy about
our lack of what they call frankness on toleration.

There is the further opportunity of collaboration
in domains outside the Faith altogether: the
mutual consideration of how best to help the
suffering and the oppressed and to further
Christian principles in the moral and social sphere.
They found it very difficult to understand when
we withdrew from the Council of Christians and
Jews, and I imagine something may now be done
to remedy this. If we feel that Anglicans have sold
the pass regarding some moral problems, there
remain many about which we agree. This is a
great opportunity for that common interest and
action which, at any rate on the personal level,
unite us more closely.

It is, of course, for our bishops, in contact as they are with the Holy See, to give us the lead and guidance in these matters which we need. It would greatly help if there were a common plan about this with common directives on a national level. Great tact and perception are necessary. For example, generally speaking the Anglicans prefer conferences and meetings on neutral ground. It is surely reasonable for them to expect suitable arrangements for their own services. On the other hand, they will not expect us to hand over our own altars and sacred vessels. And much misunderstanding, not helpful to true unity, has arisen when our Continental brethren have done this. Here we need a clear and binding international directive. Again, it is not easy to explain to our separated brethren why some of our bishops seem to take quite a different line from others regarding participation in these mixed gatherings. Above all, we need a clear and common guidance as to what prayers may be said together. Anglicans believe deeply in prayer and their enthusiasm about special prayer for unity is sometimes greater than ours. Doubtless we shall get some guidance here in the paper on Communicatio in Sacris.

One bishop recently gave me permission to address a large Anglican group in his diocese with the proviso that I should not say even the Our Father with them. Of course I complied, but the situation was embarrassing. Another bishop, in a similar case, told me to join with them in the Pater but under no circumstances to say the Apostles' Creed.

These things are a stumbling-block which our separated brethren find it difficult to understand. And they tend to draw the conclusion that Rome and the Holy Father are far more tractable than we are; and consequently turn to Italy, France, Holland and Germany for their contacts. A national secretariat in close relationship with Rome and with the full confidence of our Hierarchy could give us all much help and guidance and at the same time scotch the idea in the minds of Anglicans and also our Continental friends that we are intransigent and reluctant, or at least unco-operative. This we already have with our Bishops' Committee. Doubtless we shall see it further developed.

It seems to me that it needs perhaps a G.H.Q. to which we may all easily turn for guidance; and a full-time secretary to deal with our necessary importunities. They might eventually produce (with Rome's permission) a small authoritative manual of other prayers which might be said together in English. The Gloria, Sanctus, Agnus Dei, the Magnificat, Veni Creator Spiritus and Veni Sancte Spiritus: the great common prayers of Christendom all quite mutually acceptable. A little book of this sort might dissolve the constant anomaly and peril of withdrawing our children from the school assemblies, very often with nobody to lead them. But here I trespass on another subject. In Montréal Cardinal Leger has permitted his clergy even to read the lessons from Good King James' version at Anglican Evensong in union with the separated brethren. It is only fair to say, however, that the issue is much more clear-cut in Canada, where episcopalianism is relatively low-Church.

There are some who think that the question of Anglican orders should be reopened. Apart from the Anglo-Catholics, I have never found this to be an important issue. The ordinary Anglican clergy-man makes no claim (and has no desire) to be a sacrificing priest. Even many Anglo-Catholics take the view that the problem is a "red-herring" and that the crucial problem is the one of authority. Once the papal claims are accepted, everything else, including the expressed mind of the Church on Anglican orders, follows. In the last seventy years no important factors have emerged which could affect this judgement. Even if validly consecrated bishops (Old Catholics, for example) have participated in Anglican ordinations, the defect of form remains in the ordinal used. Any revival of the 1895–96 controversies would be deplorable. And any reopening of the question would surely raise many false hopes. If the question is brought up in our meetings we should see that it is put in the right perspective (as a corollary of authority). *Caritas et veritas*. Obviously we must acquaint ourselves with all the facts. The small group who make it their chief complaint against us usually have psychological reasons for doing so which I will not delineate here. They are the same people who would like to see an Anglican Uniate rite parallel to the mainstream of Catholic life.

This, to my mind, would only defeat the wider
purpose by irritating the main body of Anglicanism
even more. Certainly it would do so in this country
but not necessarily in the mission field, where
"monochrome" sections are to be found, like the
University Mission to Central Africa.

What else can we do to help and further our
relationship with the Anglicans? Clearly we should
all be doing something to make our own house
more welcoming and attractive. Architecturally
and artistically we are making, I think, considerable progress. We are at a great disadvantage
by virtue of our history *vis-à-vis* the Anglican possession of the pre-Reformation cathedrals, abbeys
and churches. But in the building of new churches
I would say that we are more than holding our
own: certainly in numbers, but even more im-
portantly, in standards. For the Anglican Coventry
we have the Catholic Liverpool. Generally speaking, our churches do not seem as tawdry and
repellent to the Englishman as they were fifty
years ago. Again, thanks to the decrees of the
Holy See and the response of priests and people,
there has been considerable liturgical development
on our part. This is important, because the average
Anglican is brought up in a high appreciation of
the beauty and dignity of worship. This is something which I believe derives very largely from the
strong Benedictine and monastic influences in the
medieval church life of this country. The pre-
Reformation buildings are superbly maintained
by the Church of England and the restraint and

dignity of furnishing and decoration constitute an admirable model for us all. This is the real Anglicanism; I do not speak of that small group whose passion for imitation has led them into our worst excesses. I have mentioned earlier the importance to the Anglican tradition also of really first-class church music and choirs. Our opportunities for the development of a better-class hymnology become less as evening Masses take the place of what were the traditional evening services. We can all help, however, to make our churches more attractive musically by furthering the mind of the Holy See, especially in the matter of the Missa Cantata.

It is not for me here to anticipate any disciplinary concessions that the Church may make universally regarding the vernacular. Such a concession would raise in England a problem which I think would be almost unique in Christendom; because we should have to provide translations which would hold their own with the incomparable language of the Book of Common Prayer. Whatever we may think of Cranmer, he was one of the greatest masters of English prose, providing great dignity with a great economy of language. The Englishman loves understatement. I have in my possession a small vellum volume published in Birmingham in the year of Waterloo which was a laudable attempt on the part of Fr. Peter Gandolphy to bring out a Catholic edition and adaptation of the Book of Common Prayer. I believe it was proscribed in Rome. It was

certainly conceived and born "out of due time".
But in a sense it could be a model for an eirenic
gesture in our day of considerable importance.
The problem will become easier for us, since the
Anglicans are in the process, as I have already
said, of throwing the Prayer Book overboard and
substituting new trial forms. I think we shall find,
however, that their new services will maintain
dignity and beauty of language. It is important
that we should do the same in our translations.

There is one long term and radical step which
could revolutionize and improve the relationship
between the Catholic priest and the Anglican
clergyman. It is the rethinking and rearranging of
the almost non-existent relationship between the
seminaries and the universities. This is becoming a
problem even in our own relationships. Foreigners
have often congratulated us in the past on the
happy and friendly relations between priest and
people in this country. But now we find growing
up what I can only describe as a dichotomy
between the education of the clergy and the higher
education of the laity. Each system talks its own
particular language and never the twain do meet,
(or very rarely). This situation is a breeding
ground for anti-clericalism which we would do
well to remedy. If it is true of our own people and
their priests, how much more true is it of the priest
and parson. There is in this country all too little
cultural rapport between them. The majority of
Anglican clergy have a course in a secular university behind them. Maybe this statement is less

true now than fifty years ago. But all of them have been trained in a Theological College run on English university lines. I am not saying that they have more culture or a better culture. Humanistically they probably have, but not philosophically or theologically. I speak from personal experience of both systems, and I would say here and now that no Catholic priest should ever have an inferiority complex in these matters. But he often has, and anyhow he thinks and studies and acts in a different idiom. Now, the Anglican culture is a national characteristic and the university system, however secularized, retains its ethos. Statistically, the number of practising Catholics in this country probably equals the number of practising Anglicans. But it would be a terrible oversimplification— and indeed a mistake—to say there was equality of influence. Anglicanism penetrates and touches every institution and aspect of the national life. This *Weltanschauung* is therefore important. If we are to be all things to all men we must be able to talk their language. Indeed, it is largely because of the consequent separation socially that it is so difficult to make easy contact ecumenically.

It is a great help that more of our priests are now studying in the English universities. Here the religious orders have led the way. By their houses of study in Oxford, Cambridge and London, they have made a natural impact and have certain contacts. But the secular clergy have St. Edmund's House, Cambridge. It would be fantastic to imagine that their faith has been vitiated thereby.

On the contrary, they have frequently found those formulae of relationship which the Holy Father now asks of us all. There is a movement afoot, not before it was due, to relate the seminary system more closely to the universities. I am not belittling the great work and tradition of the seminaries. One has only to recall the splendid calibre of the priests produced by Douay, Rome, Lisbon, Valladolid and the English Seminaries at home. Nor would I minimize the prime value of formation in prayer and the priestly virtues. At all costs these must be preserved. But the pastoral clergy must become more familiar with their pastures and I cannot but believe that with the right reviewing of the situation by our superiors, the two things could be combined. In addition, there is a plan for an institute of pure learning or scholarship. If these projects are encouraged they can ultimately have incalculable results in promoting an easy relationship with the English and Anglican ethos. To bring them to the truth we must penetrate their minds and translate the immutable truth of the Faith into a language they can understand.

Anglicans also have a great appreciation of scholarship, especially in the scriptural field, but also in philosophy, theology and history. We should be producing far more scholars instead of leaving it all to our Continental brethren. At the great patristic conferences in Oxford I think Catholic scholars preponderated; but hardly any of them were from this country. We have splendid material on the teaching staff of our seminaries, but owing to the wastage of man-power and the dissipation of energies in our present uneconomic seminary system, they have all too little opportunity to specialize. Speaking in general, English Catholicism has not attached enough importance to the contemplative life in the spirit of St. Thomas with his "Contemplari et tradere aliis contemplata."

What else can we do? The Church's marriage laws are, of course, a profound irritant. It is a really great sacrifice for many non-Catholics to be married in a Catholic Church. Of course we don't want mixed marriages. I can see every possible reason for hesitation in the granting of a dispensation for a mixed marriage. But once it has been granted I see no reason for not making the ceremony as acceptable as possible. And indeed, non-Catholics are frequently won over by the richness of a full Catholic wedding. On the other hand, many are embittered by the starkness of the proceedings of a mixed-marriage ceremony and resolve never to set foot in a Catholic Church again. I do not see what else we could do in this matter unless, of course, permission were given by the Holy See, as at the royal wedding in Athens, for a twofold ceremony.

Then there is the question of Communion in both kinds. I have never found this a major problem. Once an explanation of eucharistic doctrine has been given—that our Lord is present, body, blood, soul and divinity under either kind alone, and that his own twofold institution was

connected with the sacrifice—the discipline of the
Church is accepted. As the priest of a parish where
something like ten thousand Communions a
week are given, I shudder to think of the practical
prolongation and the problem of priest-power
which would arise if this concession were made.
Personally I would prefer it to be granted, if at all,
restrictively. For example, in nuptial Masses, ordinations and other like occasions. This in itself would
constitute a gesture. The important thing is for us
to keep an open mind where discipline is concerned. It is for the Church to decide.

*Truth and Charity*. We must be ready to acknowledge our faults. The Anglicans, for their part,
must be ready to forsake their errors. Nor should
we be serving truth if we were to deny the objective
history of the Reformation in this country. As the
Protestant Professor J. M. Powicke said in his
essay on this subject, "The one definite thing that
can be said about the Reformation in England is
that it was an act of State." Imposed by the Tudor
despotism, it was not the will of the ordinary people.
Equally, the Anglican Establishment was an Act of
the State created by the enactments of 1559 and the
subsequent legislation inspired by William Cecil
and ratified by Elizabeth I. Henceforth spirituali-
ties and temporalities were united in the Crown
and technically remain so. It is the Crown—in
Parliament—which rules the Church of England.
When cornered about this anomaly Anglicans will
usually answer that real spiritual authority rests
with the Convocations. No canons, however, pro-

posed by Convocation can be made effective legally without incorporation in an Act of Parliament and the subsequent royal assent. A certain practical autonomy has, however, developed. It is clearly seen in the dis-established Churches of Ireland and Wales and the relative independence of Commonwealth Anglicanism. It is clear that the present Archbishop of Canterbury is anxious to secure such autonomy for the homeland. Anglicanism is thus increasingly becoming more independent of the State. It is rather like the Siamese operation. And nowadays, I understand, there is no reason why both twins should not survive.

It is difficult for English Catholicism, in view of its history, to understand or appreciate Anglicanism, which has grown up not only in antagonism but in an incomprehensible spirit of comprehensiveness uniting nearly all the opposition, and with no philosophy and practically no positive theology of its own. But if it began and grew somewhat negatively, it has become positive by virtue of the challenge to Christendom. It is thus aware in all its sections of the necessity of unity and the scandal of a divided Christendom in the face of the atheistic and material perils of our day. This is an inestimable advance. And in this we are already united. "Where there's a will there's a way" and although it is difficult to see it, together with Christ all things are possible.

On this plane we can welcome the Anglican contacts with the Orthodox and also with the Free

Churches, the Presbyterians and the rest who are
even more cut off from us than they are. And it is
important to realize that these people form an
influence in England tantamount in some ways to
Anglicanism. We must not get it out of proportion.
In all this they have all come to appreciate and
yearn for one of the marks of the Church, viz., unity.
And one cannot help feeling that the organizations
which they have created—and of which we shall
hear more in this conference—can, under God,
prepare the way. Let us not be too impatient with
them if they sometimes put the cart before the
horse and regard experiments of intercommunion
as a means to greater unity rather than as one of
its chief ends. This is already making some of them
realize that it is only a fictitious unity which is not
based on dogmatic sanctions. The Holy See is
sending observers to these conferences and surely
this points to the attitude we should adopt.

To sum up: I have especially stressed in the first
part of this paper the importance and necessity of
individual conversions. If the Ven. Dominic had
told John Henry Newman to stay where he was,
the Church would have been deprived of one of
her greatest ornaments and countless others who
have come under his influence and inspiration—
and still do—would have been lost. The individual
convert, as he receives the gift of Faith and
responds thereto, not only plays an important part
in the salvation of his own soul and others, but also
*assists* the work of unity. He is in a unique position
to understand and break down the *obices* in others;

to welcome them in, and, last but not least, to help cradle Catholics to understand and be patient with the inexplicable vagaries of heresy, and the strange workings of the Anglican mind.

In my second part I have tried to show that at the same time we must be in dialogue with Anglicanism *as such* and I have tried to define it. Because it is nebulous and elusive we must labour endlessly to comprehend it and with our heartfelt prayers leave the rest to God. It is not for us to formulate mitigations in ecclesiastical discipline which the Church, in the spirit of charity, may accord to our separated brethren. We shall not be lagging behind her in charity, and if she asks it we shall be ready to sacrifice our own preferences, that all Christians may emerge "ex umbris et imaginibus in *veritatem*".

## 5. COMMUNICATIO IN SACRIS

*Maurice Bévenot, S.J.*

WHEN I was asked to contribute a paper on this subject, it was with some apprehension that I agreed to do so. This feeling was only intensified, when I found that such an authority as the late Canon Mahoney had found himself constrained in the last years of his life to alter his view on the very principles which had guided him for so many years in answering the questions put to him on the subject in the *Clergy Review*. After the publication of the Instruction on the Ecumenical Movement, he made an apologia, which, while it is all to his credit, reveals only too clearly how complex and intricate the problem is. In the course of a long discussion, he wrote in June 1950, vol. 33, p. 400, as his main conclusion:

> It must follow that those amongst us who have held that a united prayer with heretics . . . *is always of its nature wrong*, have been defending a too rigorous interpretation of the law in Canon 1258, an outlook due to our conditions in this country, to the traditions received from our forefathers, and to the necessity, as we conceived it, of discouraging the faithful from any religious contact whatever with non-Catholics.

He therefore accepted the opinion which Cardinal

D'Annibale had aired in 1908, viz., "Communicatio in divinis *non suapte natura* illicita est", but is forbidden by the Church owing to the danger which it is likely to cause to the Catholic religion. "Ubi igitur huiusmodi periculum cessat, recidimus in legem ecclesiasticam, cui derogare fas est, cum longe plus incommodi quam commodi habet"—"When then such danger is absent, we are left with an ecclesiastical law, which one is justified in putting aside, when it presents far more drawbacks than advantages."[1]

This fundamental change of outlook in such an authority in canon law was sufficiently disturbing to an amateur like myself; still more disturbing was the doubt that seemed to hover over the meaning of *sacra* in the expression "communicatio in sacris". The Instruction, while allowing the joint recitation of the Our Father at such meetings, required that any kind of "communicatio in sacris" should be avoided. Canon Mahoney acknowledged he was frankly puzzled. "Prayer," he wrote, "is obviously a sacred thing and the Pater Noster the most sacred of all prayers, and therefore it would seem that a joint Pater Noster, if words have any meaning, must be 'communicatio in sacris'."[2]

In subsequent correspondence, one writer seemed to accept this interpretation of *sacra*, but

[1] Art. cit., p. 399; D'Annibale, *Theologia Moralis*, 1908, vol. 1, par. 110, n. 11.

[2] Art. cit., p. 401.

suggested that there would be no technical *communicatio* if the worship was on neutral ground and not under the aegis of heretical authority; another, however, suggested that "this theological term is ordinarily reserved for the more solemn and formal services." So, the question remains: which are these *sacra*? Is the Our Father included among them or not?

If these uncertainties were already disturbing, it was with consternation that I lit upon a contradiction among the Roman Congregations themselves. The Holy Office in 1864 allowed one in danger of death to ask, under carefully restricted conditions, for absolution from a schismatic priest. Yet, to quote Canon Mahoney's note when dealing with that permission: "An earlier reply of *Propaganda*, 17th February, 1761, was in exactly the opposite sense: 'Nullo casu, neque necessitatis, licere catholico confiteri peccata sua et absolutionem obtinere a sacerdote schismatico'." [3]

With these examples in mind you will appreciate the trepidation with which I approached this subject; you will not expect from me a declaration *ex cathedra*. All I can offer you are some tentative suggestions which may lead to profitable and, I hope, not too heated, theological discussion.

Two points emerge with unmistakable clearness, and can be taken as the basis for all our efforts to find principles to guide us. The first is that at least at joint meetings we can say the Our

[3] *Clergy Review*, 34 (1950), pp. 64–7.

Father together, or some other prayer approved by the Church; the other, that on no account should we either allow non-Catholics to receive Communion from us, or ourselves receive their Eucharist. Those are the two extremes. Can we go further with our separated brethren than reciting with them the Our Father and other approved prayers, as some of the variations in the Church's practice seem to indicate? In any case, we must draw the line somewhere between the two extremes, and probably a very long way indeed before the stage of intercommunion. But wherever we draw the line beyond which we cannot go, we shall have a double task before us. We have first of all to convince our fellow-Catholics that by going that far with non-Catholics, we are not compromising the Faith. Secondly, we have to explain to our separated brethren why we can go no further with them. This is of the first importance, because it is here that most of them will blame us for self-righteousness and lack of charity.

First, then, we have to convince our fellow-Catholics that our Faith is not compromised even if we seem to be indulging in actions which have hitherto been regarded as *communicatio in sacris*.

(1) As an illustration, I deliberately take an extreme case, far from the English scene and that in the seventeenth century, concerning relations between Catholics and Orthodox. The practice of the Church then was, at least in some countries, different from our present practice, and points to the need of appreciating how much in this delicate

matter depends on circumstances and the existing attitudes between Catholics and dissidents.

Throughout the seventeenth and in the early eighteenth century, there was a number of Catholic missionaries, mostly, though not exclusively, Jesuits, working, some in Constantinople but mostly in the islands of the Aegean. There the population was mostly Greek Orthodox, and though there were a few Latin bishops the Orthodox bishops naturally dominated, and followed the directions of the Patriarch of Constantinople. In general it may be said that relations were good. Whereas the Orthodox clergy were uninstructed, the missionaries, though few, opened schools and were devoted to preaching, catechizing, and hearing confessions. The Orthodox bishops allowed them to work freely among all the people, and sometimes came to hear their sermons themselves. In the summer months, some of these Latin priests would give a series of missions in the neighbouring islands, always first assuring themselves of the good will of the Orthodox bishop concerned. Here is a short account of the methods adopted by two of these Jesuits (who were accompanied by a doctor) as reported to the Father General in 1700 or 1701.

We do not interfere with their rite—for in itself it is good and holy. We have only tried to make them observe it in a holy way, and stripped of the errors which have got mixed with it. So as not to give even the shadow of a

scandal to the weak, we adopt the Greek
practices in so far as is not forbidden. For
instance, we observe along with them the days
of fasting and abstinence which they keep. We
are scrupulous to show all due regard and
courtesy towards their ecclesiastical superiors.
We attend their services and their Masses,
which with all our hearts we wish we could sing
after their manner, in order to inspire them with
a little more reverence and recollection, which
is generally lacking during their sacred functions. As for the question of the articles of faith,
we have not failed to let them know them very
precisely and very clearly, whenever we believed
that God and our religion demanded that
they should make a profession of faith. Lastly,
the medical help that we give has been of great
assistance to us.[4]

You may be tempted to say that all this is but
another example of Jesuit laxity, playing fast and
loose with the Church's regulations. I think I am
justified in saying that the adaptations current in
these islands were simply due to the exceptional
circumstances that prevailed there, and were
approved by the Apostolic Visitors, whose often
very detailed reports have been preserved.

Thus, already, in 1652, Bernardo, a Capuchin,
speaks of the good understanding that existed

[4] G. Hofmann, "Apostolato dei Gesuiti nell' Oriente
greco, 1583–1773", in *Orientalia Christiana Periodica*, Rome,
1935, 1, pp. 139–63, especially pp. 160–61.

between the two rites [5] and again in 1667 the
Apostolic Visitor, Mgr. Sebastiani, Bishop of
Hierapolis, reports that on the island of Thira,
with only nine hundred Latins to eleven thousand
Greeks, these latter "are all well affected to the
Roman Church, and the laity are not wedded to
the schism and to the errors of the other Greeks,
but frequent our Latin Churches and go to Confession to the Jesuit Fathers, who reap much fruit
there, all of which has been much helped by the
exemplary life of our late bishop here".[6] Lastly,
though others might be quoted, in the report of
Antonio Guistiniani, Bishop of Naxos (who wrote
in 1701, the very year of the missionary expedi-
tions already described), we have an enormously
detailed description of the state of religion in the
island of Thira (Santorini).[7] The Apostolic Visitor
mentions in passing that the Latins are following
the Greek calendar, *per bonum pacis* with Greeks;
he lists the defects and slackness at the Cathedral
(where no one ever preaches except a Jesuit
brought in for the Sundays of Lent and Advent),[8]
and has a full page of encomium for the three
Jesuit priests there, who, for all their personal
poverty, are gaining great fruit of souls, in the one
rite as in the other.[9]

[5] G. Hofmann, "Vescovadi catholici della Grecia, V.
Thera (Santorino)", vol. 130 of the *Orientalia Christiana
Analecta*, Rome, 1941, pp. 56–71 (cf. p. 18).

[6] Op. cit., pp. 71–6; quotation, p. 74.

[7] Op. cit., pp. 80–106.

[8] Op. cit., p. 83.

[9] Op. cit., p. 91.

It would seem, then, that in spite of some previous decrees of the Holy Office, it was recognized that the friendly attitude of the Orthodox bishops and people in these islands justified even attendance at the schismatic services; preaching and hearing confessions in schismatic churches; and sharing churches with them. It was during the following century that things were very much tightened up—possibly in retaliation against the action of the Orthodox Patriarchs of Constantinople, Alexandria and Jerusalem, who, in 1755, in spite of the opposition of many of their metropolitans, decreed that Catholic baptism was invalid and that converts to Orthodoxy had simply to be baptized "unconditionally".[10] But I think that another cause of the tightening up was what had happened in England since the Reformation. Let me explain.

Here in England, as we all know, presence at the services in the parish church was invested by the laws of the land with a significance which was equivalent to abandonment of the Faith. The faithful did not at first recognize this, but rather made a joke of it; for them the Protestant service was just empty show. It was only gradually that the gravity of the matter was brought home to them, and then the heroic stand of the martyrs became crystallized in such a saying as that of Margaret Clitherowe: "I will not pray with you, nor shall you pray with me: neither will I say

[10] Cf. M. Jugie, *Theologia dogmatica Christianorum Orientalium*, Paris, 1930, vol. 3, pp. 111–13.

Amen to your prayers, nor shall you to mine." It
was the only possible line to take at the time and
under those circumstances, but its stark simplicity,
hallowed by the martyr's heroism, inclined people
to take it as of universal application, at all times
and under all circumstances.

So in the seventeenth century, moralists, when
they discussed *communicatio in sacris*, tended to start
with the supposition that joining in the prayers or
rites of non-Catholics was an "externa protestatio
falsi dogmatis", and only then went on to consider
in what circumstances a passive presence might be
permissible. And so, in the early eighteenth
century, the great canonist, Prosper Lambertini,
the future Pope Benedict XIV, in his *Tractatus de
Synodo Diocesana*, when summing up the different
views of theologians, puts first Paul V's Brief to the
English Catholics forbidding them to attend the
Anglican services because the King's edict decreed
that all should do so, as a practical demonstration
of their agreement with Protestantism ("ut tali
pacto se cum protestantibus sentire profiteren-
tur"). Only then does he allow for other circumstances, but says that even so, "it can hardly
ever happen in practice that *communicatio in divinis*
with heretics should not be harmful to Catholics."
("*Vix unquam accidere potest*, ut in praxi sit innoxia
catholicorum cum haereticis communicatio in
divinis.") In this way he justifies the Church's
universal prohibition in the matter. It will be
noticed in passing that he does *not* say that
attending a non-Catholic service is wrong in itself:

it is a Church law prompted by the dangers which seemed to be inherent in such action at the time.

And so in 1753 the Holy Office, in a letter to Tenos, one of the isles of Greece, forbade all *communicatio in divinis* between Greek Catholics and Greek schismatics, and for their further instruction reproduced the passage from Lambertini's work just quoted, including the reference to the English King.[11]

Thus we have an argument drawn from conditions in England in 1606, used for a decision on the situation in Tenos (such as we have seen it) one hundred and fifty years later. No doubt the decision was directly prompted by the action taken by the three patriarchs against Catholic baptism. But it seems a pity that what had hitherto been allowed in the islands, and had been to the good of all concerned, was now to be stopped—though conditions there were so different from what they were in England.

At the same time we can understand why the ban on all "communicatio in sacris" was interpreted in so wide a sense in England and perhaps extended beyond what was necessary. Let me quote from the correspondence in the *Clergy Review* which followed the permission to say the Our Father with non-Catholics. One reverend contributor wrote (among other things):

> I could not feel any more strongly than I do that *in the circumstances* in this country we should

---

[11] *Collectanea S.C. de Prop. Fide*, vol. 1, no. 389.

give grave scandal by having these common prayers. It is no use telling a crowded meeting of all beliefs and none that it is all right because the Holy Office has said we may do it: they would not have the slightest idea of what you were talking about. The scandal would still be there. The Holy Office has not, and could not have, any intention of allowing us to give such scandal as in the peculiar circumstances of this country (or are they peculiar to this country?) naturally follows on these joint prayer functions. The martyrs were not led by emotion but by solid Catholic instinct when they refused to have anything to do with such things. Let us continue to have a healthy hatred of heresy. It has been characteristic of the Church from the beginning.

This, and the various reasons alleged by the writer for the attitude which he adopted, were admirably disposed of in the next number, by Fr. St. John, whom we are so glad to have here with us. But such an outburst illustrates what Canon Mahoney had previously said about our too-rigorous interpretation of the law as being "an outlook due to our conditions in this country, to the traditions received from our forefathers, and to the necessity, as we conceived it, of discouraging the faithful from any religious contact whatever with non-Catholics".

I may here add a paragraph from Fr. St. John's reply: "No Catholic who understands what it entails can doubt that even a qualified participation in ecumenical work must be attended by dangers, but it would seem that in these days the Holy See, with its eye on the changed world situation, counts the dangers of participation under due safeguards and limitations as of less moment than the loss which might be suffered by the Church from a continued policy of isolation."[12]

The fact is that conditions *have* changed. We are quit of the artificial significance imposed by law on attendance at the services of the State Church; we have witnessed for over a century the adoption among many Anglicans, and more recently among some Free Churchmen, of many Catholic beliefs and practices which had been repudiated at the Reformation; we have, finally, the recognition, especially in the World Council of Churches, that it is possible to discuss together, to co-operate in action and even in prayer, without this signifying in any way an abandonment of one's own credal convictions or confessional loyalties.

There is less danger now of any so-called "concession" on our part being interpreted as a sign that we are weakening, or that we agree with them all along the line; and as they get to know us better, the danger should disappear. They will see that our unwonted courtesy is an expression of our *charity*, and not an abandonment of our *faith*.

In other countries Catholics have had experience of this—for instance, in Germany, at a time when Catholics and Lutherans were alike

[12] *Clergy Review*, 34 (1950), p. 144.

under pressure of Hitlerism, and today when Communism has transplanted whole populations both in the Eastern and the Western zones, Catholics into Lutheran regions and Lutherans into Catholic parts. I have heard, but have no confirmation of this, that Catholics in Russia, deprived of their own priests, attend the Orthodox services without being considered to have given up their faith. And, undoubtedly, the action of the present Holy Father has created among sincere non-Catholics an attitude of good will to the Catholic Church unparalleled since the Reformation.

In such a setting, it is proper to ask whether we are justified in perpetuating an attitude of suspicion and repudiation, which we had to take up under the tyranny of circumstances which are now things of the past? There is no question of sacrificing one iota of the Faith, there is no question of sacrificing any of the loyalty which our martyrs showed to the Holy See. Indeed, would not the martyrs today be the first to recognize that loyalty to the Faith and loyalty to the Holy See demand that we should modify our attitude towards those about us who have at least retained so much of the Christian heritage in the midst of a post-Christian and often hostile world? How far we should go is another matter.

As for the particular subject of prayer in common, we can perhaps sum up what has been said in the first part as follows: "Praying with our separated brethren may be permitted where our relations with them and the concrete circumstances are such that, in common estimation, it does *not* involve approval of the errors they may hold. What those circumstances are in the concrete must depend on prudent judgement in different places or different times."

(2) So far we have been considering what to say to our Catholic brethren who think that in fraternizing with our separated brethren we are going too far. We have now to consider our separated brethren, who complain of our intransigence as being lack of charity. This they particularly feel in the matter of prayer, and we have to bear in mind that there is great contention going on both between, and within, most of the Churches of the World Council about "intercommunion". Some hold that, as they are already united in some things, this should be manifested by united participation of the Lord's Table. Such a sharing in a common Eucharist would, they say, be an important step towards reunion, and such unity in Christ would soon break down the barriers that still separate them. On the other hand, others hold, equally strongly, that intercommunion can only be the crown of an already established unity of faith, and that to indulge in it without full unity is a desecration and a contradiction. In this, as in so much else, the Orthodox have always shown themselves as intransigent as we are, and we may rejoice that they are accustoming the other members of the World Council to a view of the Eucharist in relation to Church unity which is

indistinguishable from ours. The Orthodox are
not the only ones among them who so believe:
many Anglicans do so too and not the Anglo-
Catholics alone.

If anything is "communicatio in sacris", it is
sharing the Eucharist together, and we should at
least be able to explain why *that* is ruled out for us.
The reason is not just that Anglican Orders are
invalid, or that among Anglicans some believe in
the Real Presence and some do not—however
much those facts are relevant. We want to be able
to deal with the question without becoming
bogged down in the discussions about *Apostolicae
Curae*, about what is the meaning of the Anglican
Ordinal, about sacrificing priests and the rest.
We have to bear in mind that, in any case, the
Eucharist which they celebrate is something very
sacred to them, and that this is true of the Free
Churches too, who would never claim that they
were offering Mass. Can we then explain our
attitude in a way that they will understand—with
their existing mentality—without our directly
offending their deepest religious sensibilities?

In the early centuries of the Church, admission
to the Eucharist always presupposed an existing
unity. The public sinner was excluded till he had
done such penance as merited recognition of his
amendment and so *reconciliation* with the whole
body of the faithful. When travelling, the faithful
were given cards of recommendation by their
bishop, which assured the Churches which they
visited that they were in union with them. This

was necessary owing to the number of heretical sects, whose members could thus be recognized through lack of such *tesserae* or cards of recommendation from the bishops who shared the same communion. That these sects acted in the same way shows that the Eucharist was universally looked upon as essentially expressing full unity of faith and mutual recognition.[13]

Even these simple facts show that our attitude of "intransigence", as they call it, is not merely a hangover from the past when heretics were regarded as wicked men and even put to death. From the earliest days, the Christian attitude was not just something negative, it was the positive assertion of what was most valuable to them. Before the pagan world, the Christian martyrs appeared absurd in refusing to drop a few grains of incense into the brazier; why so stubborn and obstinate? But they felt that human salvation was at stake; there is only one God, one Saviour, one saving message, and they died in torture rather than compromise it. The mystery-cults of the day were quite open to compromise. As Professor Brilioth has written:

> The normal relation of the mystery-cults to one another was one of tolerance. Especially in the later period, the accumulation of mystic initiations was the common practice; it was prudent to acquire as many guarantees of salvation

[13] Cf. L. von Hertling, "Communio und Primat", in *Miscellanea Historiae Pontificae*, Rome, 1943, vol. 7, pp. 1–48.

as possible . . . But it was on the ground of
intolerance, from first to last, that Christianity
fought and won. It was unthinkable to partake
of the Lord's Table and the table of devils.[14]

So, too, today, all sincere Christians resist the
Hindu tolerance of any and every god, and refuse
to worship in the temples of the Mohammedans
or to share in the sacred rites of the Jews.

We may well be faced with the retort: "Then,
are Christians who differ in their interpretation of
Christian doctrine to be placed on the same footing
as the pagans of Rome, or as the Hindus, Moslems
and Jews?" Recently, Professor Peter Brunner of
Heidelberg complained that in their marriage
legislation Catholics treated the Lutherans as if
they were mere pagans, and nearer home I have
heard the same complaint because we pray for the
"conversion of England".

But if we return to the early centuries, we shall
see the positive side of Christian intransigence not
only against pagan worship but also against any
distortions of the truth about Christ or his grace.
To say that Christ was a kind of pagan demigod,
as the Arians did, was something which Christians
could not permit to be taught to the children and
ignorant people, since it undermined the substance of the Christian message. The same is true
about the early Gnostics, about the Sabellians

[14] *Eucharistic Faith and Practice*, London, 1930, pp. 53–4,
quoted by B. Leeming, *Principles of Sacramental Theology*,
London, 1953, p. 390.

who held one undifferentiated God without real distinction between Father, Son and Holy Ghost; about the Docetists, for whom Christ was *not* "like unto us in all things, sin only excepted"—which undermined the salvation of human nature as we know it. The same, too, about the Pelagians, who denied the need of grace and would have fastened on the Christian message an intolerable moralism and pride.

If, then, members of all these sects were excluded from the Eucharist of the great Church, it was because the Christians felt an obligation of *charity* to preserve the Gospel message and show disapproval of anything that perverted it. Because they loved Christ above all, they could not permit his Godhead to be called in question by subtle dialecticians; and because they loved their fellow men, they could not permit them to be deprived of that faith, or permit intolerable burdens to be placed on them, or permit the diffusion of the idea that free will emancipated man from Christ and from God. It was not merely a question of phraseologies; the different theological outlooks of Alexandria and Antioch were no insuperable barriers; Athanasius was ready to come to terms with the Antiochenes, as also did Cyril of Alexandria, notably, later on. There was a willingness to accept explanation, and to receive back those who had gone astray. What was immovable was resistance to the preaching and propagation of distorted doctrine which would falsify Christ's teaching and destroy the hope men must place in

him. And let it be recognized that if we all still
hold these fundamental Christian truths, effort-
lessly, today, it is due to the intransigence, to the
often painful intolerance, of those ancient cham-
pions of Christ.

I should like to illustrate this question of
admission to the Eucharist from an incident in the
life of St. John Chrysostom when Bishop of Constantinople. Incidentally, it brings out the relation
that was recognized to exist between the Eucharist
and the unity of the bishops and so of the Church
as a whole. Theophilus of Alexandria had not yet
launched his all-too-successful attack against
John, so that they were still in communion with
each other. But some monks and clergy from
Egypt came to Constantinople complaining that
Theophilus had grossly ill-treated and excommunicated them. John gave them an honourable
reception and even allowed them to attend Mass,
but postponed their admission to Communion
there until their affairs should be examined. The
fact was that he was still in communion with
Alexandria, and had he at once admitted to full
communion those who had been excommunicated
by their bishop, it would have meant a breach of
relations with Theophilus. At the same time no
formal accusation against them had, it would seem,
reached John from Alexandria, and so he saw no
reason for treating them as entirely outside the
Church.[15] However, his prudent action did not

[15] Cf. Von Hertling, art. cit., p. 17, and Socrates, *Church
History*, 6, 9.

prevent a false rumour reaching Theophilus that John *had* admitted them to the Eucharist, and Theophilus set about securing John's deposition. Here we have an instance where no matter of faith was in question, but where the disciplinary unity of the Church was shown to be intimately bound up with joint participation in the Eucharist.

Such examples may help to show our separated brethren that it is not arrogance or lack of charity which moves us when we put limits to our readiness to co-operate with them: we feel that there are greater things at stake. Nor should they have great difficulty in seeing it; for if I am not mistaken, Evangelical Protestants and Anglicans would feel insuperable difficulty in receiving communion at our Mass, or in reciting, with Catholics, prayers to the Virgin Mary or to the saints. This would not indicate lack of charity on their part, but only their conviction that the Catholic Church is mistaken in these very fundamental points and that they must not act in a way which might suggest that they had given up their conviction about "Roman errors and superstitions". Thus Professor S. L. Greenslade has said that he would himself "have to overcome at least as much prejudice against communicating at a Roman Mass as any Anglo-Catholic would have against communicating in a Calvinist Church".[16]

(3) These very general considerations, mostly drawn from the past, may not solve our immediate

[16] "Intercommunion: A Personal Opinion", in *Intercommunion*, London, 1952, p. 229.

problems, but I think they form a useful back-
ground for deciding what we should do in practice
today. More immediately, we are faced by two
sets of facts. *On the one hand* there seems to be a
very general agreement that separated brethren
are, as we say, "in good faith" that is, that
Orthodox, Anglicans, Protestants generally may
err in faith without formal sin against the Faith.
Moreover, there is a very wide consensus among
theologians that separated brethren possess true
Baptism, true (though imperfect) faith, and many
other Christian values. Under the circumstances,
the problem about "communicatio in sacris" must
involve not only the question of approval of false
doctrine, but also the question of apparent *disapproval* of the truths which separated brethren
have in fact preserved.

*On the other hand* stand the mistaken theories
about the nature of Christ's Church which are
held by many Anglicans and Protestants. Among
some is the idea that everyone who "commits
himself to Christ" is a full member of Christ's
Church—which is equivalent to the theory of an
invisible Church. Closely allied to this is the idea
that all Christians are in fact united to Christ, and
all that is wanting is the *manifestation* of this unity.
Lastly, there is the theory—which is widely held—
that the Church of Christ is like a rock which has
been broken up into pieces, larger or smaller—
each of which retains some at least of the qualities
of the true Church, but none of which is the whole
Church. Reunion will make the whole Church

appear. I must add at once that, more often than not, these theories are held unconsciously and unformalized. But it is clear that they influence those who press for intercommunion among Anglicans and the Free Churches, at least on special ecumenical occasions.

The matter, therefore, is a delicate one: whether approval of the true Christian elements may seem to be approval of false theories about the Church; or, on the other hand, whether manifested disapproval of false views (by refusal to share in prayers, etc.) may seem to be disapproval of true Christian values.

We must admit that the situation at present is unprecedented and new in the history of Christianity, and that methods adopted in the past need not be the best methods today. What is new and unprecedented is *not* the existence of heresies, nor the effort to recall heretics by argument or persuasion, but the common admission that friendly relations do not involve any surrender of principle. This has been manifested in the experience of the World Council of Churches over some fifty years, and has been enshrined by them in the Toronto Declaration. It has been manifested again in the almost universal welcome which the present Holy Father's openheartedness, in word and act, has met with in the non-Catholic world, and in particular in the visits which Archbishop Fisher, the Moderator of the Church of Scotland, and so many others, have paid to him.

On the other hand, we have to bear in mind the long tradition that has prevailed in this country, in Ireland, in Australia, and in the United States. A long tradition is one thing; the reasons for the practice it represents are another. We may think that those reasons no longer hold good; but a long tradition is a fact, and cannot be altered in a day. So we have to remember the possibility of *scandalum pusillorum*, until such time as by instruction and example that danger is removed, and the only obstacle left on this side is *scandalum pharisaicum*.

Our conclusions can only be tentative, general, and feelers rather than proposals:

(1) It would seem that, if we make our position clear—as we can—a larger measure of common prayers does not present danger of seeming to approve heresy.

(2) Our position has for so long been restrictive that modifications of the restrictions should be gradual and prudent. (Even Canon Mahoney, as long ago as 1944, could envisage such prudent modifications. Thus, on the question of a Catholic teacher in a non-Catholic school forbidden to attend the morning act of worship, he wrote: "If it is thought that the time has come for a modification of this law and practice, the matter is for the judgement and direction of the local Ordinary.")[17] Today he would perhaps have said: "The time *has* come."

[17] *Clergy Review*, 24, 1944, p. 185.

(3) (If it needs mentioning at all)—there can be no question of "intercommunion". But I do not think this is likely to arise in any case. I cannot imagine the Orthodox allowing anyone, even ourselves, to come to their communion—even if we wanted to. And the British Council of Churches have even been contemplating drawing up a service which would emphasize *abstention* from communion, with a view to encouraging people to work for real unity.

(4) There seems no reason to prevent a Catholic priest from accepting an invitation to speak in a Protestant Church. It has been done more than once, and only good has come of it. But I think he should make clear, before accepting to do so, that he cannot return the compliment—however ungracious this may seem.

(5) It should be possible to make a distinction between what is generally permissible, and what can be allowed to individuals on certain occasions. I have in mind the possibility of Catholic "observers" being allowed to be present at a meeting held under the auspices of the British Council of Churches, and also such meetings between theologians as the one soon to be held at Worth. In the first case, the "observers" might perhaps attend a service in a non-Catholic Church; and in the second the Catholic theologians might do the same (if the guests of non-Catholics), and in any case might have prayers in common with them on a larger scale than it would be wise to allow to the faithful in general. There is a special reason for this

in the latter case. The very nature of a dialogue involves entering into the mind of the other party (so far as is possible), so as to see how, precisely, he sees things, how it compares with one's own view, how much one can approve of, and how one can express one's own faith in a way that the other party will understand. The process is a difficult and often painful one, and presupposes a solid knowledge of the Faith, without which it would be distinctly dangerous. It would seem that theologians who are chosen for this sort of work could likewise attend and join, say, in Evensong with the Anglicans, and thereby learn something of their prayer in practice, which, after all, is at most deficient rather than erroneous. This they could do without danger to themselves, without misleading those present and, please God, as the faithful are better instructed in the ecumenical spirit, without scandal to the faithful who hear about it.

(6) Lastly . . . and here I have no suggestion to make, because my subject plays only a subordinate part in a greater whole. This greater whole is the keeping of the Unity Octave, kept sporadically only, up and down the country, and hardly ever, so far, under Catholic auspices or initiative. Perhaps it is more natural that it should be so, but where it has not been kept so far, the question may arise whether the Catholic clergy should promote it themselves. There is the question of the public meeting with a common platform, or whether it would not be best to have separate

services in the churches of the different denominations. At a public meeting the question of prayers together arises, and I for one have been impressed by the anxiety the others have shown to confine themselves to what we are specifically allowed. There is the fact that the World Council of Churches puts out a leaflet with appropriate Scripture readings and prayers for each day of the Octave. I know that at least this year they were vetted by a Catholic priest in the Secretariat for Unity, Fr. Michalon, so that they could be used by Catholics too. There is the devoted work of Fr. Keldany in distributing the Octave leaflets. And there are the Friars of the Atonement, whose special work is promotion of the Octave. All these and many other aspects of the problem would seem to call for special attention, perhaps for a special committee which amongst its other tasks would have that of considering the point where "communicatio in sacris" impinges on the Unity Octave.

# 6. THE WORLD COUNCIL OF CHURCHES

*Jérôme Hamer, O.P.*

DURING this talk I shall speak about the World Council of Churches in the main lines of its present evolution. But I hope in the discussion to be able to read you some of the declarations made yesterday and the day before at Paris in the course of the business of the Central Committee of the World Council of Churches (August 7–17th). These declarations concern the relationship of the World Council of Churches with the Second Vatican Council. Why are we interested in the World Council of Churches? It is certainly not for its spectacular side nor yet for the sake of its influence on international bodies, e.g. U.N.O. We are interested in the World Council of Churches because it works for Christian unity. We are interested in it not only for the work it does, but for what it represents as a sign of a new mentality.

The separation of Christianity into different groups with different confessions is no longer considered irrelevant by the theologians of the Protestant Churches today. New-Testament scholarship has shown that the Church is one in God's plan and that a plurality on the local level can only be the plurality of manifestations in different places of the one Church. It is in this sense that Church law will name a particular

Church when designating a certain diocese. At the beginning of his two Epistles St. Paul is careful to state that he addresses the Church *in* Corinth, not the Church *of* Corinth. This clearly demonstrates the unity of the one Church in spite of the diverse local manifestations. New-Testament scholarship shows, too, that the Church is visible.

From this it follows that there is a clear tendency to fight diversity and scattering, e.g., merging of Christian bodies, as seen in the Church of South India. There are similar schemes for union being suggested for North India and Nigeria. Very often these mergings are based on principles that we cannot accept, e.g., doctrine, creed, Church order. But, nevertheless, they reveal a desire for unity.

A large part of the Protestant world is abandoning in a certain measure that spiritual individualism which reached its worst forms sixty years ago in the time of modernism and liberalism. And it is discovering, more and more, the meaning and function of the Christian community in the plan of salvation. At the same time it is discovering that that community must be universal, according to the will of Christ. It is this new mentality that will explain the creation and the development of the World Council of Churches.

You are specialists in ecumenical questions, so it is unnecessary to go into details, but may I remind you of a few major facts? The World Council of Churches is composed of 197 Churches from all the different parts of the world, except China. It is composed of big Churches and small ones; and of different confessions. An important fact to bear in mind is that the Patriarchate of Moscow, with several other Orthodox Churches from that part of the world which is actually dominated by the Communists, is a full member of the World Council of Churches.

In Edinburgh in 1910, in a great missionary conference, the absolute incompatibility between the various divisions and real missionary endeavour was experienced. Two movements emerged from this, one working towards a practical Christianity, the other focused more on doctrine and ecclesiastical order. Then the two movements fused, provisionally in 1938, definitely in 1948. We have heard a great deal about the big assemblies of the World Council of Churches, Amsterdam in 1948, Evanston in 1954 and New Delhi in 1961. A special significance marked the New Delhi meeting. A new link was forged here with the International Missionary Council.

It is not easy to analyse such a new and complex reality as the World Council of Churches. Should one approach it through its norms or laws or from the practical point of view? I propose to look at both sides. On the one hand we have the Constitution (accepted in 1948, revised in 1961) and some official explanations about the nature of the World Council of Churches and its objectives (the Toronto Statement, the New Delhi Statement). On the other hand, there is the interior evolution of the World Council of Churches, its many activities and its institutional changes, such as the integration with the International Missionary Council. As it is impossible to give a complete view of the whole we shall have to confine ourselves to studying only typical points of these two aspects:

1. The Basis
2. The New Delhi Statement
3. Integration.

These three points form the divisions of my talk.

## 1. THE BASIS OF THE WORLD COUNCIL OF CHURCHES

The text as revised in 1961:

The World Council of Churches is a fellowship of Churches which confess the Lord Jesus Christ as God and Saviour, according to the Scriptures, and therefore seek to fulfil together their common calling, to the glory of one God, Father, Son and Holy Spirit.

(A) "The World Council of Churches is a fellowship of Churches."

This implies that it is not a Church. It exercises no authority on any of the member Churches. It makes no laws nor does it control actions. Its only authority is the wisdom of its own decrees and its acceptance by the Churches. The doctrinal documents that it issues have no value in themselves. Their only value is that given them by the Churches which decide to accept them. The

World Council of Churches does not have its own
eucharistic worship. Why? Not only because of
the practical impossibility of having a service
acceptable to all (Baptists, Reformed Churches,
Lutherans, Anglicans, Orthodox) but by de-
liberate choice. The Assembly, as such, has no
eucharistic service. The reason is that it cannot
appoint a minister who would have the authority
and power to celebrate the sacrament. There is a
new proposal being seriously studied—that is, to
refrain from all celebration of Holy Communion
during the time of the Ecumenical Conference.
But in fact the statement (that the Council is not
a Church) is not as hard as it sounds when we
consider other things. The World Council of
Churches has the following functions: "To express
the essential unity of the Church", "To manifest
the essential unity we have in Christ." Such
sentences come spontaneously from the language
of the World Council of Churches. They are not
considered theological statements, but they have
theological implications. It is obvious that to
manifest the unity we have in Christ is an essential
function of the Church. This is what brings us to
another point.

The World Council of Churches has nevertheless some elements of a Church. "It fulfils some
functions of a Church which are not fulfilled by
the separate Churches. For instance, it expresses
their universality, as none of the individual
member Churches can. It bears a common witness
and renders a common service in the world, as no

individual Church is in a position to do. And most important of all, it is regarded and understood from outside as a unit—to a far greater extent than it regards itself as such." (L. Vischer, in *Ecumenical Review*, 1962, vol. 14, p. 290.) So we shall not be surprised to see that some Protestant theologians (Van Dusen, for instance) deem that the World Council of Churches has at least as much right to be called a Church as any of the historical Churches. Also, in its teaching functions, the World Council of Churches has a tendency to a certain independence. The resolutions it adopts have validity for the individual Churches only in so far, and as long as, those Churches accept them. But in fact, "Resolutions are adopted from which the individual Churches can hardly dissociate themselves. This means that in reality the World Council of Churches is becoming an independent factor, distinct from the Churches." (L. Vischer, op. cit., p. 283.)

We ought also to indicate another fact which clearly shows a certain tendency of the Council to act like a Church. Within some quarters of the World Council of Churches there is a growing tendency towards intercommunion. One should add that this is met by strong opposition from the Orthodox Church. It is based on the conviction that a conference gathered in the name of Christ may be regarded as a temporary and local expression of the Church. So we read in a recent article: "So the solution is perhaps in the acceptance of intercommunion in certain circumstances, in the framework of the ecumenical meetings." (M. Thurian, in *Verbum Caro*, 1961, no. 57, p. 45.)

(B) "The Lord Jesus Christ as God and Saviour."

There is a real progress of the new phrasing in relation to that of Amsterdam (1948). There are two major additions: " . . . according to the Scriptures" and "to the glory of the one God, Father, Son and Holy Spirit". The first addition was initiated by a bishops' meeting of the Church of Norway. The second was repeatedly put forward by influential circles in the Orthodox Churches and came also from other quarters, including the General Council of the Congregational Churches of the U.S.A. "The basis should be made more explicitly trinitarian in character." (*St. Andrews, Minutes of the Central Committee*, p. 211.) The World Council of Churches does not consider those additions as coming from new and foreign elements, but as pure explanations, the result of development of the original idea. "The expression does no more than make explicit what has all along been implicit in the present basis." (*St. Andrews*, p. 212.) The Basis is not a creed. The Catholic friends of the Ecumenical Movement were happy to read the new phrasing of the Basis. They saw in it an enrichment of the faith; nevertheless there must be no misunderstanding. We cannot compare this text either with the baptismal profession of faith or with the definition promulgated by the ancient Councils. It is not a creed, a confession, a full statement of the Christian faith. But it is more than a mere formula of agreement. It is functional. Its sole purpose is to state, for the member Churches, what holds them together in the World Council, what is the starting-point of their consultation and the foundation of their collaboration. (*St. Andrews*, p. 211.)

I would like to insist on the fact that it is not a creed by comparing it with the Nicene Creed— a symbol of faith. A creed is first of all a profession of faith, the act of a Christian who personally accepts the word of God who saves him. It is also a *regula fidei*, a standard of pure doctrine and of orthodoxy. For this reason a profession of faith is required from all converts. It is also imposed upon all bishops when they are consecrated. The Lutheran confessions have this character. A creed may also have a liturgical significance. The summary of our faith may become an element of our official worship, because the creed sums up the history of our salvation.

From each of these aspects, the confession of faith is always an act of the Church as such. This is not the case with the Basis.

(C) Views and Attitudes Concerning the Basis.

Every Church desirous of joining the World Council of Churches should examine itself seriously to see if it can take part in a union resting on this precise Basis. Each Church must decide for itself if in all sincerity it can support the doctrinal Basis. The World Council of Churches would exceed the

limits it has imposed on itself, if it tried to judge
whether a Church was faithful to the doctrines
laid down.

The new Basis was accepted at New Delhi.
There have been some explanations of the votes.
Professor D'Espine declared that the Federation of
the Protestant Churches of Switzerland wish to
safeguard the doctrinal liberty customary in the
Swiss Churches. Pasteurs Westphal and Gaillard
of the National Synod of the Reformed Church in
France said that they "accept the new Basis as an
attempt to express the mystery of God's revelation
without seeking to impose any particular theology
on the member Churches". 383 voted yes to the
Basis, 36, no, and 7 abstained. What surprises
Catholics very much is that not one Church that
voted against the proposal has left the World
Council of Churches. We may conclude that the
acceptance of the Basis is not a duty imposed on
each of the particular Churches, but that the Basis
belongs to the *operation* of the World Council of
Churches as such. It is the constitutional foundation of the Council's *activities*. This is a very
important distinction which is often forgotten.

Is there not a social link, a principle of cohesion,
besides that of the Basis? A close consideration of
the life and activities of the World Council of
Churches will gradually give us the answer to that
question. But already there is a very revealing fact.
Recently three Churches of South Africa have
spontaneously left the World Council of Churches
because they felt that their adherence to racial

segregation was incompatible with their membership. It would seem, therefore, that there are
ethical, as well as doctrinal, principles within the
interior cohesion of the World Council of
Churches.

## 2. THE NEW DELHI STATEMENT

The principal documents which try to express
the nature and the purpose of the World Council of
Churches are the Toronto Statement (1950) and
the New Delhi Statement (1961). What is the
nature of these documents? They are not parts of
the Constitution, but theological essays, papers to
be submitted to the member Churches for close
consideration.

The purpose of the Toronto Statement was to
explain the nature of the World Council of
Churches to those who fear that it could become a
kind of world Church. The first assertion is very
clear on this point. "The World Council of
Churches is not and must not become a super-
Church." But this is chiefly a negative aspect. The
positive aspect was emphasized by the doctrine of
"Vestigia Ecclesiae". We shall return to this in our
discussions.

The intention of the New Delhi Statement was
to show the kind of unity to which the World
Council of Churches directs its work, especially its
department of "Faith and Order". In an earlier
draft that paragraph was preceded by a preface
which reads as follows:

The Faith and Order Movement was born in the hope that it would be, under God, a help to the Churches in realizing His Will for the Unity of the Church . . . We have become convinced that the time has come for a fuller statement of this purpose.

The New Delhi Statement reads as follows:

We believe that the unity which is both God's will and his gift to his Church is being made visible as all in each place who are baptized into Jesus Christ and confess him as Lord and Saviour are brought by the Holy Spirit into one fully committed fellowship, holding one apostolic faith, preaching the one Gospel, breaking the one bread, joining in common prayer, and having a corporate life reaching out in witness and service to all and who at the same time are united with the whole Christian fellowship in all places and all ages in such wise that ministry and members are accepted by all, and that all can act and speak together as occasion requires for the tasks to which God calls his people.

That document was very largely approved in New Delhi, even by the Orthodox. This is a new and interesting fact. From the Catholic point of view, we acknowledge that all the elements mentioned here are quite authentic. We only claim more. We are looking for what is missed out. Moreover, we can only appreciate the text within the framework of a historical development. Therefore a comparison between New Delhi and Toronto may be useful. I see progress in the greater importance given to visibility. If the World Council of Churches holds on firmly to this ideal, it will have to amend some parts of the Toronto Statement.

The New Delhi Statement is centred on visible unity. It is not satisfied with a purely spiritual or invisible unity, nor yet with a purely federal unity that is, an external association of autonomous groups. This visible unity requires one ministry, one body of doctrine, one sacramental life. Toronto, on the contrary, declared: "The World Council of Churches cannot and should not be based on any one conception of the Church. It does not prejudge the ecclesiological problem . . . Membership in the World Council of Churches does not imply the acceptance of a specific doctrine concerning the nature of Church Unity." And the commentary on this sentence states all the possible concepts of unity, not forgetting the following: "Those who conceive the one Church exclusively as a universal spiritual fellowship or hold that visible unity is unessential or even undesirable . . . [The World Council of Churches] includes Churches which believe that the Church is essentially invisible as well as those who hold that visible unity is essential."

I think that the New Delhi Statement, in relation to Toronto, is simply a natural development arising from thirteen years of experience of practical fellowship within the Council. But at the

same time it demonstrates a real and clear progress, which actually amends the former statement
on a major point. To correspond to the new
situation of the World Council of Churches, the
Toronto Statement requires a serious revision.

Where are the limitations of the New Delhi
Statement? They are to be found principally in
the question of the ministry. The question of the
legitimacy of the ministry accepted by all is
central. The authors know it very well and therefore have added a commentary which stresses that
difficulty:

> All agree that the whole Body is a *royal
> priesthood*. Yet one of the most serious barriers to
> unity is our diverse understanding of the nature
> of the ministry within the corporate priesthood.
> All who have been engaged in church union
> negotiations testify to this fact. There are those,
> for example, who affirm the necessity of an
> episcopally ordained ministry in the apostolic
> succession, while others deny that it is essential
> for the true Church. How can two such
> divergent positions on so important a matter
> be settled? In this, as in all matters relating to
> Christ's Church, it is upon the Holy Spirit we
> must rely.

In this context, the Catholic theology emphasizes rightly the apostolic succession, in which
it sees the mission of the Apostles, carried on by
the episcopacy, directed by Peter's successor.

### 3. The Integration

To have a complete view of the World Council of Churches we should consider its varied activities. Very often Catholic theologians tend to identify the whole of the World Council of Churches with the work of one of its departments, "Faith and Order". This is a big mistake. Here are some of its activities: Help for Refugees, Inter-Church Aid, Commission on International Affairs, Ecumenical Institute of Bossey, Work Camps, co-operation in the realm of evangelism. But, as I have said, I wish to limit myself to a major fact: the integration of the International Missionary Council with the World Council of Churches.

The International Missionary Council groups together the missionary societies; to be more precise, the national and regional councils. In reality it is a Council of Councils. Among its purposes, we know that it has to encourage evangelism; to co-ordinate the activities of various missionary bodies; to seek to unite Christian public opinion in support of freedom of conscience, including liberty of worship.

The first impulse came from that same missionary conference in Edinburgh in 1910. The ecclesiological significance of the integration has been clearly explained by Dr. Visser 't Hooft, general secretary of the World Council of Churches, in 1958, at the Central Committee which met in Denmark at Nyborg Strand. Here is a summary of his position. In 1948, in Amsterdam, the two fundamental ecumenical concerns were brought into vital relationship with one another. The main arguments used in those days were very largely of a practical nature. As long as Faith and Order and Life and Work went their separate ways, there was too much overlapping and waste of energy. But the real motives went much deeper. Both movements stood for unity; the one for visible unity in faith and order; the other for fellowship in service to humanity. Now it has become increasingly clear that these two aspects of unity cannot be promoted independently. There are dangers on both sides: a self-centred unity, lacking the proper dynamics and remaining unconvincing, or a sentimental and superficial unity. So the covenant made in 1948 meant that the World Council of Churches was committed to a movement "which would not minimize the serious doctrinal issues of unity, but which would seek to work at these issues in the setting of the common calling of the churches to humanity". So the unity the World Council of Churches stands for may be called a *pastoral unity*. "A unity not merely for the sake of the Church but for the sake of mankind."

If the World Council of Churches had realized that unity in the framework of the common calling, it could never feel satisfied with only an indirect relationship to the central task of the Christian Church which is its world-wide mission. And so integration is the inevitable consequence of the choice made in Amsterdam. On the other hand, the same spiritual logic had been operating in the world missionary movement.

The member Churches are working in the World Council of Churches for the pastoral missionary unity which is indicated in the Scriptures. This has a consequence for the activities of the World Council of Churches. To end disunity is not the only *raison d'être* of the Council. Such activities as the propagation of the Faith, the relief of want, the struggle against injustice, belong to the same purpose of pastoral unity. Working in these different practical fields, the World Council of Churches is helping to bring into being that spiritual situation between the Churches without which unity is inconceivable. So far the summary of Dr. Visser 't Hooft's report.

This study of the 1948 decision which led to the 1961 merger throws into relief a fundamental aspect of the unity which is the purpose of the World Council of Churches. That unity, that purpose, gives to all its activities its specific note.

Let us sum up what we have said up to this point, by drawing attention to an important double distinction.

(1) We must distinguish carefully between what the World Council of Churches says about itself, and what it is in fact. This is true anyway of every society, whether religious or secular.

(2) It is also essential to distinguish sharply between what the Council says about the Council and what it says about the Church.

Keeping this before our eyes we can state:

(*a*) The basis of the Ecumenical Council plays an important but nonetheless, relative and limited role. There are other elements which are sociologically effective as factors of unity within the World Council of Churches.

(*b*) The Toronto Statement concerns above all the interior unity of the Ecumenical Council. It determines the theological conditions for fruitful "co-existence". This determination is, moreover, more negative than positive.

(*c*) The New Delhi Statement concerns the unity of the Church, as it exists as the ultimate goal of the World Council of Churches.

(*d*) The declarations on "pastoral unity" made in connection with the recent integration concern at the same time the unity of the Church and the interior unity of the Council, the first conditioning the second.

## Conclusion

### *The World Council of Churches at the Crossroads*

It would indeed be a poor lookout for unity if the World Council of Churches were to stand still in its evolutionary process and fix itself as a static organization. This would be a sorry solution, a catastrophe. Were this to happen, the World Council of Churches would be acting as a Church perhaps without assuming the name "Church".

We have to remember that some Protestants, especially in the United States, would be satisfied with a certain kind of loose federation in a framework of real practical co-operation. Unity theological problems belong, for some of them, to the academic level. Those problems are not practical enough, not "real" enough. Where would the danger be? I do not think that the World Council of Churches will try to impose doctrinal statements, but it could, if it became a static body:

(a) Accept the idea of intercommunion as its own.

(b) Take over certain responsibilities in missionary work, in the sense that the World Council of Churches would do its own missionary work.

But the dangers are still far off. "Faith and Order", tradition and the pressure of the Orthodox will certainly stop this possibility from being realized at the present time. I emphasize here the influence of the Orthodox Church. At New Delhi the Orthodox representatives acted as a body on the doctrinal level. That gives more importance to "Faith and Order". Let us note the fact that the Russians intend to work specially on the "Faith-and-Order" level.

The World Council of Churches may work as an educator of the sense of unity. It may lead people to a truer idea of unity and, we may say, it is already working in that direction:

(1) By drawing attention to the radical dif-

ference between the "denomination" and the
Church as it is portrayed in the New Testament.

(2) By showing how the visibility of the Church
is a necessary trait. This is done by showing that
the flight towards the spiritual and invisible is
unfaithful to the institution of Christ and a retreat
in the face of the true problem. It is just this escape
which is always a hidden and often unconscious
temptation for the Protestant world.

(3) The third way is by spotlighting the
necessary universality of the Church, as a communion which is universal and indispensable, and
which has to be a real not a merely superficial
union; a real communion and not only "intercommunion".

(4) Fourth and lastly, it may help the different
Churches to see their way clearly in the dialectic of
diversity and unity. On this point a reassuring
fact came to my notice during a recent stay in the
United States. A Church leader, who represents
a large majority of the American Protestants,
made a statement to me which I shall try to
summarize: "A certain amount of diversity
may be useful. It helps to cultivate a variety of
spiritual gifts. Some diversities in theological
explanations, liturgical practice, hymnody . . .
may be helpful. But certain deviations in doctrine,
order and conduct would wound the Church and
betray its Christian mission. Some of those
varieties may depart from the very essence of
Christianity, faith in God, in Jesus Christ, in the

Trinity, in the reality of the Atonement, in the Church." I take that statement as marking real progress in the way of unity and as a happy result of ecumenical confrontation within the World Council of Churches.

## 7. THE BRITISH COUNCIL OF CHURCHES

*Bernard Leeming, S.J.*

I SEIZE this opportunity to add my word of thanks to His Eminence Cardinal Bea for coming here and for his regular attendance at our meetings when he must be pressed with many matters of vital importance, and when what we say must often seem very elementary to him. I owe him, likewise, a personal debt of gratitude for his patience with me when he was my Superior in Rome and for his encouragement in my early teaching days at the Gregorian University.

There are undoubted risks in entering the ecumenical dialogue; but there are far greater risks in trying to stay out, or in allowing vague fears to engender a half-hearted attitude which makes the worst of both worlds. If we look for a sign from God, I think we may find it in the complete agreement of Dominicans and Jesuits on this matter—clearly both have received a *praedeterminatio physica* securing this agreement.

Secondly, I would like to endorse the desire of many Catholics, if not of absolutely all, for more opportunities of praying with our separated brethren. My reason for this is that it is difficult, if not impossible, to explain either to our own Catholics or to non-Catholics the divergences about what is permitted and what is not. I do not think that common prayers will solve the problems of disunity; but I think that a more open attitude would greatly help to dissolve some of the non-doctrinal factors in our divisions. Of these, as they exist in Northern Ireland, Professor R. P. C. Hanson has written as follows:

There is a well-known story of a Protestant supporter of a Protestant football team in Belfast coming away from a match in which the opposing team (Roman Catholic) had been defeated, and murmuring, "There'll be sore hearts in the Vatican the night!" This story, like all genuine myths, may not have happened, but it could easily have happened. In Northern Ireland disagreement in religion contributes to a host of other differences, and these in their turn contribute towards the aggravation of that disagreement; according to your religion you choose the games you play (hockey, for instance, and cricket are Protestant, but hurley and Gaelic football are Catholic), the dances you go to, the newspapers you read, and (of course) the politics you profess. Both sides, Protestant and Roman Catholic, have by now become thoroughly and (one is tempted to say) impregnably vested interests. The buying of land, the determining of political wards and constituencies, the politics of local authorities are complicated by religious allegiances, and in their turn emphasize and exacerbate denominational differences. So deeply ingrained is this

particular division that there is little doubt
that, were every soul in Northern Ireland to
become by some psychological alchemy a
Moslem over night, the country would continue to be divided into two camps without the
slightest lessening of animosity. It should
perhaps be added that the demand for reunion
among the non-Roman Catholic Churches in
Ireland is more often than not based on the
quite untheological desire to present a stronger
and more united front to Rome. [*The Summons
to Unity*, London, 1954, p. 59.]

Professor Hanson wrote in 1954, and things may
have changed somewhat in Northern Ireland since
then. At Maynooth in 1961 the delegates from
Belfast made the most moving pleas for greater
charity. Conditions, of course, are different in
different parts of England and Wales. But I am
convinced that to pray together on suitable
occasions will have a definite effect in helping to
dissolve non-theological factors in divisions, for
prayer together is bound to make us all more
humble and more docile to the inspirations of the
Holy Spirit of love and of unity, Christ's own
Spirit.

Thirdly, I should like to express gratitude to our
Continental Catholic brethren who have blazed
the ecumenical trail. For over thirty years I have
known of a certain divergence between English
and Continental Catholics; and I think that people
like Portal and others have occasionally shown

themselves neither omniscient nor all-wise. On the other hand, neither have we English Catholics always been completely wise. W. G. Ward, with what Chesterton has called his "apocalyptic absoluteness" and "ferocious clarity", to some extent influenced subsequent writers and helped to exacerbate the controversy with Anglicans and to perpetuate "war-psychology" and to create an image of us as a minority group soured by centuries of persecution and almost unwilling to extend the courtesies of life to those of other beliefs. But all English Catholics owe incomparably much to Continental scholars like Archbishop Jaeger, and Sartory, Hoefer, Boyer, Bouyer, Tavard, C. Dumont, Le Guillou, Baum, Congar, De Lubac (whose book *The Splendour of the Church* is so moving), Algermissen, Jedin and Fransen on Trent, Dvornik on Photius—to mention only a few. Perhaps some of us are a bit influenced by our English insularity and inclined to agree with what Bill Bobstay said of Ralph Rackstraw in *H.M.S. Pinafore*:

> He is an Englishman,
> For he himself has said it
> And it's greatly to his credit
> That he is an Englishman.
> For he might have been a Roosian
> A French or Turk or Proosian
> Or perhaps Itali-an.
> But in spite of all temptations
> To belong to other nations
> He remains an Englishman.

It would be not only scandalous but disastrous if our separated brethren were to feel that there were permanent divisions among Catholics, and although we may think that some of our Continental brethren have occasionally acted without consummate wisdom, still we owe them on balance a very heavy debt for their theological and ecumenical learning, solidity and perspicacity, and a magnanimous acknowledgement of this plain fact will help to draw us completely together. (Cf. "The Abbé Portal Then and Now", *Heythrop Journal*, 2, no. 4, Oct. 1961, pp. 345–55.)

One other preliminary observation: If we engage in ecumenical activity, we must expect to suffer. If it is the cause of Christ then we must expect to suffer persecution, for the devil is sure to oppose with subtle attacks. We must be prepared for misunderstandings, charges that we are too weak or perhaps too fierce, that we compromise the Faith or jeopardize it by unwise defence. Sometimes there may be information that we cannot disclose and we may have to suffer in silence. So at the beginning, make up your minds to suffering and don't be surprised when it comes. His Holiness John XXIII has said that the only triumph we seek is the triumph of Christ and his cross, and perhaps that triumph must begin in us and only through his cross in us can the triumph be extended to others.

Now for the British Council of Churches—we refer to it as the B.C.C. which is easily confused with the B.B.C.!

*History.* It is an amalgamation in 1942 of the British section of the World Conference on Faith and Order, the Council on the Christian Faith and the Common Life, and the Commission of the Churches for International Friendship and Social Responsibility.

*Presbyterian)?*

*Its Members* include the main ecclesiastical groups; Anglicans, Baptists, Congregationalists, Churches of Christ (Disciples), Methodists and Moravians, in England, Scotland, Wales, Eire and Northern Ireland (with the exception of the Baptists in Scotland and Wales and of certain groups of independent Methodists). All its member churches are likewise members of the World Council of Churches.

"Participating in the work of the Council" have been the Salvation Army, the Quakers, some Unitarian and Free Churches, the Y.M.C.A., the Y.W.C.A. and the Student Christian Movement.

The Inter-Varsity Fellowship, an "evangelical" association, strong in certain universities, does not participate; nor do the Plymouth Brethren, the Pentecostals, the Adventists, the Lutherans, the Free Church of Scotland or the Union of Welsh Independents.

*Its Purposes Are:*

(*a*) To draw the churches represented on the Council into greater understanding and unity.

(*b*) To enable the churches more fully to share in the Ecumenical Movement.

(c) To enable the Churches to bear a more united witness in the community and to serve it more effectively.

(d) To give such expression to their common faith and devotion as may from time to time be found desirable.

*Its Basis*. Up to 1961, this has been acceptance of "Our Lord Jesus Christ as God and Saviour".

At New Delhi in 1961, the World Council of Churches expanded its Basis to read: "The World Council of Churches is a fellowship of churches which confess the Lord Jesus Christ as God and Saviour according to the Scriptures and therefore seek to fulfil together their common purpose to the glory of the one God, Father, Son and Holy Spirit."

The Faith and Order Department of the British Council, at its meeting in March 1962, was unanimous for accepting the expanded Basis, except for the representative of the Friends, Dr. Maurice Creasy, who thought that many Quakers might feel that the expanded Basis looks too much like a confession of faith, and that, although the Quakers would accept the doctrine, some would find difficulty in its formularization. The matter was left for further consultation with the Quakers.

When "local councils" were formed in some towns, the Unitarians were not invited, which offended them.

The British Council, though it has never explicitly said so, accepts the famous Toronto Statement of the World Council of Churches, the main sense of which is that no church in any way compromises its ecclesiology by membership; on this ground, the Orthodox, who hold that they alone are the one true Church of Christ, are members of the World Council.

The British Council is in close touch with the World Council, distributes its literature, is represented at its meetings and may be said to be a branch of the World Council.

The British Council is also in touch with the Conference of British Missionary Societies, which includes some thirty-eight member groups and twenty-two societies or organizations "specially admitted". Some of these missionary societies, but not all, were members of the International Missionary Council, now amalgamated with the World Council under the title of the Division for World Mission and Evangelism. The connection of the British Council of Churches with the Missionary Conference does not seem very close, though they co-operate in Inter-Church Aid and Service to Refugees. Among the Missionary Societies, the heaviest contributors to the funds of the Conference are the Methodists, the Church Missionary Society (Anglican "Evangelical"), the Society for the Propagation of the Gospel (Anglican "high"), the London Missionary Society (Congregationalist) and the Baptist Missionary Society.

*Its Plans*, in general, are inspired by the awareness that the insights of the leaders of the ecumenical movement have not yet reached the ordinary clergy and church members. The plans are mainly three:

(*a*) Increase in number of "local" councils, of which there are at present about two hundred in different parts of the country though only six are listed in Scotland, nine in Wales and three in Northern Ireland. Information is lacking about the activities of these local councils. In some towns they have organized a procession on Good Friday ending at one church with appropriate hymns and sermon. Some organize meetings to encourage prayer during the Octave in January.

(*b*) Conferences at the local level in different regions of the country to discuss and digest the definition of the goal of the ecumenical movement given by the Faith and Order Commission of the W.C.C. This reads:

We believe that the unity which is both God's will and His gift to His Church is being made visible as all in each place who are baptized into Jesus Christ and confess Him as Lord and Saviour are brought by the Holy Spirit into one fully committed fellowship, holding the one apostolic faith, preaching the one Gospel, breaking the one bread, joining in common prayer and having a corporate Life reaching out in witness and service to all and who at the same time are united with the whole Christian fellowship in all places and all ages in such wise that ministry and members are accepted by all, and that all can act and speak together as occasion requires for the tasks to which God calls His people.

Five booklets for study purposes have been prepared, dealing with aspects of this definition; only two as yet are available in print:

God's Will and Gift, by J. G. Davies

Making it Visible (Questions Pertinent and Impertinent), by G. B. Caird

All In Each Place, by A. H. Dammers

Witness and Service To All, by R. C. Mackie

In All Places and All Ages (Studies in Catholicity), by R. E. Davies.

Also available shortly:

New Delhi To Britain, by R. C. Mackie, with Bible study notes by John Weller

Towards Unity, by Hugh Martin, specially suitable for beginners.

Annotated book lists are being provided by the British Council of Churches to give guidance for additional reading.

It is hoped that these meetings will prepare for what is called "an ecumenical breakthrough"; and the importance of Britain is emphasized, as being the place where many divisions began and still a kind of "homeland" of many, especially in Australia and the U.S.A.

(c) A Faith and Order Conference at Nottingham from September 12th to September 19th, 1964. The preparations for this have already been detailed as regards numbers—some 550—and accommodation. But the nature of this "ecumenical breakthrough" is not defined, beyond the general statement that the aim is "to act together in all matters except those in which deep differences of conviction compel us to act separately". It is hoped that the regional conferences may indicate ways and means likely to help towards the ultimate union of the Christian bodies in Great Britain.

Catholic "observers"? Mr. John Weller, Secretary of the Faith and Order Department told me that they would in general welcome participation by Catholics. Granted that there is no objection in principle to the presence of Catholic "observers", the question arises whether the time and energy would be well spent, compared with the other calls upon a busy priest's time.

An answer to this question depends upon the good which might be accomplished, which in turn depends upon an estimate of the state of these non-Catholic bodies and the part that Catholics could, in the concrete, play in our mutual search for complete unity amongst us.

*Judgement about Churches*

Appraisal of non-Catholic religious bodies in Great Britain is difficult, for it should include:

(a) Some estimate of the numbers of church

buildings, of church members and "adherents", of the extent to which these latter actually participate in church life, and of the hopes of union based on sound principles.

(*b*) The help given in money and manpower to foreign missions.

(*c*) The works of charity and of civic responsibility in which its members are engaged.

(*d*) Their general influence, through the spread of ideas and outlooks in the country.

*Statistics*

Statistics about religious membership are unreliable and may easily be misleading.

(1) The figures supplied may be wrong, v.g., the total figures supplied by denominations in certain countries, when added up, have exceeded the total population.

(2) There are different methods of reckoning "members", "adherents" and "total community"; some give all the baptized as members, others only the baptized and confirmed, others only "adults"— and it may be feared that some give as part of the total community those who visit a place of worship only rarely.

(3) From year to year, or period to period, different methods of computation may be used by various bodies. Government census may be unreliable, for a variety of different reasons.

(4) Mergers of churches, v.g., South India and the United Church of Christ in the U.S.A., may

draw off considerable numbers from the parent bodies; new names of countries, v.g., Ghana, and new geographical boundaries, v.g., Poland, Germany, make assessment more difficult.

(5) Figures ought to be comparative to the growth of the general population and to the growth of other religious bodies; but this is exceedingly difficult. There seems, however, general agreement that the number of Christians in the world is relatively decreasing due to the rapid increase of population in lands predominantly non-Christian.

(6) Statistics from countries behind the Iron and Bamboo Curtains are practically impossible to obtain; v.g., in Poland, the "break-away church" claims numbers varying from 100,000 to 400,000.

Accurate statistics, however, can be of the greatest use in planning for the future, and even in deciding policy; demographic surveys and sociological studies are approaching the strictly scientific and producing most valuable results. To fill out forms is a truly apostolic work in these modern times of rapid social change. For instance, Gerhard Lenski, in his *The Religious Factor, A Sociological Study*, New York (Doubleday), 1961, finds that 30% of Catholics in Detroit marry non-Catholics and that 14% of the Protestant partners later become Catholics, whereas only 27% of Protestants marry non-Protestants. The fact for instance, that 70% of Detroit Catholics attend Mass at least once a week may be of importance in planning the size of churches. Similarly, the planning of school buildings depends upon accurate statistics about population increase.

The following indications are taken from the *World Christian Handbook*, World Dominion Press, for 1957 and 1962; *The Year Book of American Churches* for 1961 and 1962; *Facts and Figures about the Church of England*, Church Information Office, 1962; *The Episcopal Church Annual* for 1960, More-house-Barlow, New York; *The Catholic Almanac* for 1961, Doubleday, N.Y. distributor; John Highet, *The Scottish Churches, A Review of Their State 400 Years After The Reformation*, London, 1960; Kenneth Slack, *The British Churches Today*, London, 1961; and *Christianity Today* (a neo-evangelical periodical published in Washington, D.C.) in its issue of 20 July, 1962. The indications, therefore, in no sense pretend to be exact or comprehensive.

## Numbers of Protestants

| | Catholic Almanac 1961 | World Christian Handbook 1962 |
|---|---|---|
| Africa | 6,795,262 | 18,986,113 |
| North America | 72,212,961 | 72,535,843 |
| Latin America | 2,576,223 | 9,029,439 |
| Asia | 9,195,623 | 28,370,418 |
| Europe | 113,572,145 | 126,331,432 |
| Oceania | 8,598,357 | 8,428,253 |

As regards Africa, Asia and Latin America the differences are striking; as regards North America, Europe and Oceania there is not a very great difference. For the total number of Protestants (including Anglicans) the *Catholic Almanac* gives 212 million plus, the *World Christian Handbook* gives 263 million plus, a difference of over 50 million.

## The Larger Denominations

The *World Christian Handbook* for 1962 gives the following figures as claimed:

| | |
|---|---|
| Lutherans | 72,588,559 |
| Baptists | 50/60,000,000 (adult membership 24,065,952) |
| Anglicans | 38,500,000 |
| Presbyterian and Reformed | 45/50,000,000 |
| Methodists | 42,500,000 (adult membership 19,086,420) |
| Congregationalists | 6,000,000 (adult membership 2,250,000) |

Taking the highest figures, the total number of Protestants in the world would be 264 million, divided as about 227 million in the larger denominations and some 37 million in the smaller groups and "the sects". Since 1957 the total increase is claimed—by some authorities—as about 8 million; but I reckon that of these at least 5 million are in the United States, and only 3 million in the rest of the world. It is obvious that in the world outside the United States the increase is not keeping pace with the increase in population, or even with the natural increase to be expected from the total number of Protestants and Anglicans. My reckoning, of course, may be mistaken, but *Christianity Today*, an "evangelical" publication, speaks most alarmingly about the decline both in numbers and in practice of the denominations in "Free Europe" and roundly pronounces that Europe is now "a mission land". Dr. Robert P. Evans, an American resident in Europe, judges that not over 5% in West Germany attend church with any regularity.

*Great Britain*

There is much evidence that all the non-Catholic churches, during the last sixty years, have declined in numbers, in church attendance and probably in influence, but that from about 1950 the decline has lessened and that a resurgence, perhaps as yet slight, has begun.

In the Church of England, infant Baptism went down from about 700 per 1,000 live births in the country in the 1920's, to 600 or less in the 1950's, the curve steadily descending. Confirmations, from 1885, declined from about 375 per 1,000 of the population over 15 years of age to 282–315 between 1948 and 1960, the decline definitely less during the last ten years. As to the number of clergy, the Rev. Kenneth Slack, general secretary of the B.C.C., in *The British Churches Today* (S.C.M. Press, 1916), says:

It is estimated that in 1901 there were some
23,670 clergy in the provinces of Canterbury
and York. In 1921 there were still 22,579. In
1951 there were only 18,196. Even more striking
is the fact that today there are 3,263 persons to
every clergyman below the age of 65. In 1901
there were only 1,570.

Ordinations, however, in 1951, were 411, but in
1960 were 601; in 1959 the entrants to the ministry
almost equalled the losses. Since 1950 the curve
seems upwards, the average age of candidates
decreasing and the number of university candidates
slightly increasing.

Whether Easter communicants are any guide
may be doubted, especially in these days of travel;
for what they are worth, however, in the Church
of England, the records show a definite decline
from 1920, when there were 94 per 1,000 of the
population over 15, to 1940, when there were 54
per 1,000; but since 1948 the curve has risen
steadily each year to 1958 when there were 68 per
1,000. Parochial expenditure, however, ever since
1908, has steadily fallen relatively to the value
of money, and the proportion given to foreign
missions has also fallen—from 8·9% in 1908 to
only 3·4% in 1958.

Sunday-School attendance has fallen almost in
proportion to the increase in the number of motor
cars, a decrease probably affecting all churches.

The Church of England, however, is showing
distinct signs of adaptability to modern conditions,

in increase in youth clubs, adult religious education, chaplains in factories, marriage advisory councils and similar matters.

As regards the Free Churches, the Rev. Kenneth Slack, in his account of British Churches, has a heading: "Nonconformity's Glory and Decline", in which he says:

> The decline in membership of the Free Churches has been great. It is normally recognized that the Baptist Churches have particularly reliable statistics, since membership of them is based upon so definite a personal confession of faith. In 1906 the membership is given as 434,741, in 1957 it was but 327,048. Even more steep was the decline in the number of Sunday School scholars. In 1906 it was 590,321. In 1957 it was little more than half that figure— and the rate of decline was accelerating. At the time of the Methodist union in 1932 there were 838,019 members of societies. In 1959 there were only 733,658. The Congregational Churches, which were most closely allied with political Nonconformity, have perhaps naturally suffered most of all. In 1909 they had 456,613 members. Fifty years later that number had sunk to 212,017. During the half-century the population of England and Wales grew from 32,527,843 to 43,758,000. [pp. 71–2.]

Numbers, however, are by no means the whole story. In Scotland, for instance, Dr. John Highet

estimates that the percentage of members who
attend church at least once on Sunday is about
63 of Roman Catholics, Baptist 78, Methodists
63, Congregationalists, 49, Episcopal Church, 40
and the Church of Scotland, 34. Thus, in Scotland,
Baptists seem better churchgoers than Catholics.
Things, of course, are very different in England,
Wales, Eire and Northern Ireland, but I have the
impression that the members of the Free Churches
are becoming more fervent, if less numerous. In
biblical scholarship they have produced scholars
of the calibre of H. H. Rowley, C. H. Dodd,
Vincent Taylor, Christopher North, N. H. Snaith,
L. H. Brockington (to whom several students of
Heythrop are heavily indebted), G. Henton
Davies, Aubrey Johnson, Theodore Robinson—
to mention only some who spring to mind. The
*Baptist Quarterly* maintains a high standard of
scholarship and forward-looking churchman-
ship; one of the best books on liturgy, *Call to
Worship*, is by an ordained Baptist, the Rev.
Neville Clark. The liturgical year is more and
more being observed; the Eucharist is holding a
more central place in worship; there is a wider
charity, a less introspective attitude, and the
problems arising in modern times about the
reconciliation of congregational autonomy and
combined Christian action are being worked out,
slowly perhaps, but surely. The cleavage between
"liberal" and "fundamentalist" is gradually
closing. Free Churchmen are among the most
trusted and most capable among the leaders of

the Ecumenical Movement; and in the British Council of Churches, men of different nations, English, Irish, Scotch and Welsh, and of different traditions and different denominations, work together with a sense of being engaged in a common cause for Christ.

Undoubtedly the most encouraging sign is the renewed interest in the Christian faith among students at universities; to this chaplains of all denominations bear witness. There is, however, some evidence that the Students' Christian Movement, which is non-denominational, is losing ground to the denominational associations and to the Inter-Varsity Fellowship, which is "evangelical". The divergence here, by Mr. John Lawrence's account in *The Hard Facts of Unity*, S.C.M. Press, 1961, is the old "liberal"/"fundamentalist" issue.

## World Denominationalism and Ecumenism

The influence of the Churches in Britain, and the question of their possible reunion, cannot be separated, on the one hand, from the associations on a world scale of the different groups: the Anglican Communion, the Lutheran World Federation, the Presbyterian World Alliance, the Congregationalist World Conference, etc., and on the other hand, from the World Council of Churches, which works for Christian consolidation on universalistic principles and on a basis of the truth of the Incarnation and of the Trinity. Both these two factors deeply influence the position of the churches in Great Britain. The world denominational associations disclaim any separatism; at the same time they tend to give greater confidence to their members and their organizations in all countries, by fostering a sense of wide expansion of the denomination. Their structure is purely consultative yet their influence is considerable and is growing. Leadership, to a large extent, both in the world denominational associations, and in the World Council of Churches, comes from the United States, though it must be said that the Americans have been singularly self-effacing and generous. One of the largest bodies in the Protestant world is not a member of the World Council, namely, the Southern Baptist Convention, though some of its leading members are showing sympathetic interest.

## The Religious Boom in the U.S.A.

In the United States the proportion of the population affiliated to Churches has steadily risen—from 16% in 1850 to over 63·4% in 1959. In the last ten years the Protestants increased in numbers by 15%, while the general population increased by only 13½%. Dr. Henry Van Dusen, President of the Union Theological Seminary, New York, says in an essay in *The World Christian Handbook*:

> The most acute observer of the American scene, Professor D. W. Brogan of Cambridge University, recently reported: "Religion in the

> U.S.A. like many other things, is booming . . .
> That there is a genuine religious revival, I do
> not doubt. That churches are not in retreat,
> I do not doubt."

And one of the foremost American churchmen,
Dr. Eugene Carson Blake, in an article in a
popular journal, under the caption "The Current
Boom in Religion" commented:

> Yes, the boom is upon us—a religious
> resurgence, a move back to God, a re-
> awakening—it's here. The evidence of a
> quickened interest in religion is beyond chal-
> lenge. We have already cited instances of
> increased membership. Church attendance,
> church construction, church giving, the publica-
> tion and sale of religious books, religious themes
> on cinema, radio and television—all are at
> unprecedented levels. The most heartening and
> significant feature of this spiritual upsurge has
> been that nowhere have the tides of religious
> concern flowed so deeply and powerfully as
> among young Americans, especially in the
> universities, with their consequent enlistment
> in unprecedented numbers for life service in
> church vocations. [*The Church in the U.S.A.* . . .
> 1961, op. cit., pp. 51–2, quoted by kind per-
> mission of the World Dominion Press, through
> Mr. H. Wakelin Coxill.]

Whereas in Europe three main types of Protestant tradition prevailed, Lutheran, Reformed
and Anglican, in America these number only

one-fourth of church membership, and three-fourths are found within denominations of "Free Churches", which originated mainly from the English Independents. There is great emphasis on religious liberty, on personal religious experience, and considerable mistrust of any centralized authority; these churches tend to be "activistic", or perhaps missionary, greatly interested in the "social gospel" (sometimes caricatured as "do-goodism"), and have a passionate desire for Christian unity. Only about three million are Episcopalians, though their influence is greater than their numbers might suggest; and hence, to a considerable extent, the influence of the Church of England and the churches in Britain as regards episcopacy may prove, likewise, greater than the numbers of church members. The Church of South India numbers only a million and a half at most; yet its influence has been very great. Any effective plan to unite episcopal and non-episcopal Churches in Great Britain would also have an influence wider than numerical considerations might suggest.

### Catholic Observers at Regional Meetings?

The Secretary of the Faith and Order Department of the British Council of Churches indicated to me that Catholic participation at regional meetings would not be unwelcome. As such meetings, however, are of an informal character, any invitation would come from the organizers of the local meetings.

Should such invitations be extended the case for acceptance may be put thus:

(1) There are precedents: Catholic "observers" at Oberlin, 1957, St. Andrews, 1960, New Delhi, 1961; the many semi-official meetings of Catholics and others in the United States, Canada and Australia, as well as in Europe; and the presence of non-Catholic "observers" at the coming Vatican Council. It has been made clear on all sides that this mutual concern for one another excludes any idea of compromise of doctrine or any suggestion of "bargaining" as regards Christian faith and practice.

(2) The presence of Catholics would be an encouragement to efforts to overcome divisions which are such a scandal to unbelievers.

(3) The Catholics observers might be able to help towards understanding and unity between various groups; a Catholic doctrine often acts as a "catalyst", and the clearness of Catholic doctrine generally may well prove a help.

The work, however, will be slow and difficult, requiring disinterestedness, humility and patience. There are unquestionably presuppositions against much Catholic doctrine. Our claim to be the one Church of Christ is regarded as arrogant; we are suspected of demanding liberty when we are in a minority and denying it when we are a majority; our outlook and faith is thought to be unduly "authoritarian" and even intolerant; and the Papacy, the Mass and devotion to the Mother of

God are unacceptable to many, if not all. On
the other hand, there is growing understanding of
Catholicism, manifest in books by writers such as
Macafee Brown, Jaroslav Pelikan, E. Skydsgaard,
George Lindbeck, Donald Baillie, and a good
many others associated with the World Council;
and use might be made of the reports from Lund
and New Delhi and the reports of the theological
commissions of the W.C.C.

Pastoral problems and the devotional life may
well be matters of common concern; and there
seems no reason to assume either a "defensive" or
an aggressive attitude or tone. If there are presuppositions against us, they can best be met by
evidence of humility, good humour and helpful-
ness. The time spent may not be repaid in
spectacular results; it may be wearying and
monotonous, but it is God's work, and with the
blessing of obedience we can embark on it with
serene confidence.

## 8. CONCLUDING REFLECTIONS

*(in translation)*

*Cardinal Bea, S.J.*

SINCE it has been decided that I ought to speak to you in Latin, I am doing so. But I have no orders to give you, nor even any exhortations to any particular action. I intend only to make suggestions for your consideration.

We sang our Te Deum this evening, and with good reason—for this conference has been richly blessed and most useful.

(1) Useful, first of all, to me, and I am sincerely grateful to have been able to be present among you. Personal experience of the differing conditions in different places and countries is invaluable. Without such knowledge, the Secretariat for Promoting Christian Unity can be of small use. I have never been in England before and I have learned a great deal. So the Conference was most useful to me.

(2) Useful, also, for all of you. This appears to have been the first great official occasion for ecumenical discussion between priests and religious from every diocese and all parts of the country. Our meeting was a true "dialogue" and not a monologue. One thing which has impressed me is that conditions in various parts of England and Wales are distinctly different, and require methods a little different. Granted that conditions do differ,

there are, nevertheless, some general norms which are of universal application. Some of these became clear in the course of the Conference, and when you return, you will be able to inform your bishops or superiors of what went on, so that the whole Hierarchy may know what transpired and what is required. Thus the conference will prove fruitful for all dioceses and for the whole of England and Wales.

I shall not repeat what has been so excellently said by the experts who addressed us, but shall merely mention one or two main matters which stand out.

(a) You will naturally expect me, as an old Professor of Scripture, to speak of scriptural matters. The Bible is our common possession, and for our separated brethren it is the origin and foundation of all doctrine and piety; it is likewise, though the fact is sometimes not realized, the foundation of all our own doctrine and piety.

The encyclical *Divino Afflante Spiritu* gave impetus and encouragement to the biblical movement amongst us. It is not needful for everyone to be engaged in philological and critical studies, but all can and must appreciate the importance of the doctrinal content of Scripture. In England, the biblical movement can do great good and ought in every way to be fostered and strengthened, and perhaps a Biblical Association, as in other countries, established.

The Secretariat for Promoting Christian Unity drew up a statement on "The Word of God" for the Central Commission of the coming Vatican Council. The document was accepted.

(*b*) The Liturgy, likewise, is of the greatest importance. We know of the liturgical spirit and practice among Anglicans, and without doubt it is a real apostolate to carry out all services with great reverence and dignity. The people must be still more earnestly encouraged to share in a living way in Holy Mass, and, as far as possible, to follow the Liturgy in their missals. Sermons greatly help if they explain the meaning of the sacred actions and prayers, and of the feasts of the liturgical year. The liturgical movement is not a fashionable fad, but something to be taken by us all with great seriousness. The instructions given us in *Mediator Dei* and *De Musica Sacra et de Sacra Liturgia* should be explained and put into practice.

(*c*) Dialogue with separated brethren is necessary and must be encountered with them on the theological level. It ought to be well prepared and undertaken only by competent theologians, always with the explicit or tacit approval of the Hierarchy. We ought not even to seem to impose our doctrine upon separated brethren. A real dialogue is sought, not a monologue; but, at the same time, the Catholic should be able to show that our doctrine is really founded in Scripture and ancient tradition.

Dialogues on pastoral and devotional matters can also be fruitful. We all have the same interests at heart—devotion, faithfulness and obedience to Christ; and we have at heart the fostering and deepening of a true religious life among our separated brethren. For this purpose pastoral dialogues are most useful, as actual experience of them between French Catholic bishops and Protestant pastors has shown.

Should we leave Protestants to themselves, almost with the hope that they will dissolve and disappear? Such an attitude would be most unchristian. Far from desiring this, our attitude ought to be one of joyful readiness to help them to make their own religious life effective, and to let them have every possible assistance from our pastoral experience.

(d) The laity often complain that they are not sufficiently esteemed and that their help is not welcome. We must not allow them to get the impression that we regard them as a lower order in the Church; their assistance, especially at the higher intellectual level of university life, can be invaluable, as experience shows.

Here, in passing, I add that I most heartily endorse the desire expressed by Mgr. Wheeler that the intellectual formation of the clergy should be better cared for. The constitution *Deus Scientiarum Dominus* provided that theological studies should be on the same high level as secular studies. It is much to be desired that here in England, future priests should be able to obtain degrees in a theological faculty, that is, in an institution of university standing and requirements. This, of course, is the concern of the Hierarchy, but, as a member of the Congregation for Universities and Seminaries, I will do everything in my power to help to this end. Priests must be in no way inferior to the laity in learning or intellectual standards and attainments.

Returning, however, to the laity, every effort must be made to fill our students with sound knowledge of their religion and with an apostolic spirit. The setting up of the Commission for the Laity is no empty gesture, but a well-considered effort to present to the coming Council the needs of the laity and their true position and function in the Church.

(e) What has been called "the apostolate of the Press", which nowadays includes radio and television, deserves intelligent and assiduous attention. This attention should be paid not only to strictly religious books, periodicals and newspapers but also to publications of all kinds. A polemical tone is useless, but serene statements, with due care to give the Press accurate news, ought to be issued after collaboration between competent clergy and laity. As you know, the Secretariat for Public Relations has been set up to provide information about the Council, and has plans for other publications when the Council is over.

## The Spirit of Work for Unity

(a) I repeat that charity and truth are the essentials. But it may be apposite to insist that if we act in charity so also must we act in truth. The guiding principle must be Catholic doctrine. No means ought to be accepted or advocated which

are not fully in accord with our doctrinal position.
There are real dangers in an eirenicism which can
approach to indifferentism. Care must, therefore,
be taken to make practice always fully accord with
the doctrine we hold and must explain.

(*b*) Balance is needed in ecumenical activity.
Many matters are not yet clear, and it would be
useless to discuss them. But it is clear that all such
activity must be directed by the Church and by
the Council.

In preparation for the Council, questions have
been put about religious liberty, work for unity,
mixed marriages, "communicatio in sacris", the
language of the Liturgy, prayers for unity, and the
apostolate of the laity. All these questions have
been considered with great attention, have been
discussed and will be further discussed. There is
every hope that the Council will probably publish
a directory about the matter. The Instruction of
1949 spoke of conditions then existing, but much
water has flowed under the bridges since then.

Guidance from the Church will not be lacking,
and it will be the concern of the Hierarchy to
apply directions to local conditions. This is the
function of the Committee for Unity of the
Hierarchy which has been appointed. On the other
hand, personal initiative is also needed. Laws do
not act, but people. The best of laws count for
nothing, unless they are put into practice with
prudence, constancy and energy. Priests must be
brought, through sound instruction, to grasp the
high importance of this question of unity, so that

they may make use of every opportunity with prudence and resource.

Small meetings of the clergy may prove of great benefit. Such can be held with the consent of the Hierarchy and with the help of some experienced and competent priest. Perhaps, as has been done in parts of the United States and in France, a diocesan secretary might be appointed to undertake the general advancement of the work, especially the encouragement and guidance of the clergy. Yet the clergy and laity ought to seize any opportunities that offer and ought not to wait for orders from authority. Each individual ought to be aware of his own personal responsibility, a responsibility which he himself has before God, the Church and his neighbour. Conscious of his responsibility he ought to act, whenever action is possible.

(c) Balance is needed in the choice of ways and means in ecumenical activity. Activity ought not to be governed by a restless desire for novelties and rejection of the fruits of experience. Methods tried and proved ought to be followed. Conditions, indeed, in the British Isles are different from conditions elsewhere, and full account must be taken of this. At the same time, on the Continent there has been considerable experience and in the British Isles much can be learned from this experience. Books have been written, from which much help can be gained. I mention, in passing, the books of Frs. Tavard, Gregory Baum, Boyer, Congar, Dumont, Bouyer, and Michael and other

Catholic laymen. The Anglican Bishop Stephen
Neill's writings can also instruct and help you.
Among the most useful periodicals are—*Istina*,
*Vers l'unité chrétienne*, *Unitas* (both in its English and
French editions) and the *Herder-Korrespondenz*.
Those who write in these periodicals, like the
authors of the books mentioned, give us the fruit
of their experience. They can help you greatly,
but, of course, some few matters need adaptation
to conditions in these Islands.

(*d*) Unity among us Catholics is needed, and
indeed is essential. This, of course, does not mean
that we must all, as it were, "follow the Party line",
since differences of view may even prove helpful;
but such differences of view must not impede our
common action. Furthermore, it is not wise to air
such differences too freely in public: "In necessariis unitas, in non necessariis libertas, sed
maxime, in omnibus, caritas"—in necessary things
unity, in things not necessary freedom, but above
all and in all, charity.

(*e*) Patience, finally, is of supreme importance.
What has gone on for centuries cannot be undone
in a few years. The divisions between Christians,
with their sad consequences, have lasted for
centuries. So we must advance one step at a time,
looking wisely to see what is here and now possible
and what must be put off till better times. Intem-
perate haste can only defeat our own purpose.

The first apostles had to convert the whole
world. But to convert the Roman world took four
centuries, and there were many setbacks. So, too,

it is in our own undertaking. One thing is clear: the Spirit of God works in all the baptized and we have evidence of his action. What we learn about the World Council of Churches, about the British Council of Churches, what has been done, written and spoken about unity—all this proves the activity of the Holy Spirit. His activity is, indeed, mysterious. Pope Benedict XV, approached by the initiators of both the Faith and Order and the Life and Work movements, refused co-operation. Pope Pius XI, in *Mortalium Animos*, was not encouraging. Yet, today the presence of Catholic observers at World Council Assemblies is an accepted fact. The Holy Spirit works among separated brethren as well as among us. It is for us to follow his guidance and to co-operate, each in his way, each according to his capacity. We plant and water, but he who gives the sun, the rain and the dew, and through these the growth, is God.

It follows, then, that our main and fundamental means will always be to pray daily "that all may be one", and with our prayers to join sacrifices— in other words, reliance must be placed on supernatural means, and this because, as I said in the beginning, all unity, whether or not it be conversion—individual or collective—is a grace of God. All this Christ, our Lord, taught us through his priestly prayer which he poured forth at the Last Supper, and through his passion, which began that same evening. Such conviction about the supernatural nature of the work will give us patient and courageous endurance of difficulties and of lack of success, and will remind us of St. Paul's words: "Now I rejoice in my sufferings for your sake, in my flesh I complete what is lacking in Christ's afflictions for the sake of the body, that is, the Church." (Col. 1.24.)

So, Your Grace, my lords, reverend fathers— my brethren in the priesthood—I end by recalling those other words of St. Paul: "It is my eager expectation and hope that I shall not be at all ashamed, but that with full courage now as always, Christ may be honoured in my body, whether by life or by death." (Phil. 1.20.)

# ECUMENICAL BIBLIOGRAPHY

English language books and review articles normally accessible. * = non-Catholic.

### A. History and Constitution

* *A History of the Ecumenical Movement 1517–1948*: Rouse and Neill: S.P.C.K.

*The Churches and the Church*: B. Leeming, S.J.: Darton, Longman & Todd.

*Two Centuries of Ecumenism*: Tavard: Burns & Oates.

* *The Ecumenical Movement*: N. Goodall: Oxford University Press.

### B. Catholic Ecumenism

*Essays in Christianity*: H. St. John, O.P.: Blackfriars Publications.

*Christian Unity. Maynooth Lectures*: McNamara: Maynooth Furrow T.

*That They May be One*: Gregory Baum, O.S.A.: Bloomsbury. (Documents.)

* *Documents on Christian Unity*. 3 Vols.: Bell: Oxford University Press. (Vol. 3, 4th series most important. Documents.)

*Christian Unity and the Ecumenical Movement*: C. Boyer, S.J.: Faith and Fact Series, Burns & Oates.

*Catholicism and the Ecumenical Movement*: Todd: Longmans.

*The Ecumenical Movement*: G. Weigel, S.J.: Geoffrey Chapman. (Woodstock Papers.)

*The Ecumenical Council and the Laity*: Cardinal Bea and Joint Pastoral of Dutch Bishops: Paulist Press.

C. *Eirenic Theology*

*Christ, Our Lady and the Church*: Y. Congar, O.P.: Longmans.

*Approaches to Christian Unity*: Dumont: Darton, Longman & Todd.

* *Spiritual Authority in the Church of England*: E. C. Rich: Longmans (a convert).

*The Spirit and Forms of Protestantism*: L. Bouyer, S.J.; Harvill.

D. *Towards understanding non-Catholic positions*

* *The Hard Facts of Christian Unity*: John Lawrence: S.C.M. Press.

* *No Apology*: John Wilkinson: Darton, Longman & Todd.

* *Christendom*: Einar Molland: Mowbray (an account of all Churches).

*Christian Denominations*: Algermissen: Herder (similar to the above).

E. *The Different Christian Traditions*

* *The Protestant Tradition*: J. S. Whale: Cambridge University Press.

* *Modern Catholicism*: Walter von Loenwich: Macmillan. (Lutheran view of the Church.)

* *The Riddle of the Roman Catholic Church*: Jaroslav Pelikan: Hodder & Stoughton. (Lutheran.)

* *Twentieth-Century Christianity*: Stephen Neill: Collins.

F. *The Eastern Churches and the Ecumenical Movement*

* *Vision and Action*: Prof. L. A. ~~Landes~~ Zander: Gollancz.

*Christian Churches of the East*, vol. 2, *The Dissidents*: D. Attwater: Bruce Publishing Co.

### G. Dialogue

*Where Do We Differ?*: G. Weigel, S.J.: Burns & Oates.

*Catholics and Protestants*: Christiani and Relliet: Sands.

\* *The Unfinished Reformation*: Asmussen and others: Fides Publications.

\* *The Spirit of Protestantism*: Brown: Oxford University Press.

### H. History

*Ecumenical Councils*: H. Jedin, O.S.B.: Nelson and Herder.

*The Church in Council*: E. I. Watkin: Darton, Longman & Todd.

*The General Councils of the Church*: F. Dvornik: Faith and Fact Series. Burns & Oates.

### Review Articles

"Can Unbelievers Be Saved?": C. Davis: *Clergy Review*, May 1962.

"Faith and Dissident Churches": C. Davis: *Clergy Review*, April 1959.

"Cardinal Newman and Uncreated Grace": Stephen Dessain: *Clergy Review*, April and May, 1962.

"Is Newman's Theory of Development Catholic?" H. Francis Davis: *Blackfriars*, July and August, 1958.

"The Authority of Doctrinal Development": H. St. John, O.P.: *Blackfriars*, Oct., Nov., Dec., 1955.

"Bible and Tradition": H. St. John: *Blackfriars*, July and August 1958.

"A Suggestion about Inspiration": D. J. B. Hawkins and the Abbot of Downside: *Downside Review*, July 1962.

The above are only a few selected articles dealing with subjects of ecumenical importance. The following reviews all carry a number of articles of ecumenical interest. They are generally accessible bound, in various libraries in seminaries and religious houses. They are all worth consulting *passim* for the past dozen years.

*Unitas*
*The Eastern Churches Quarterly*
*The Heythrop Journal*
*The Downside Review*
*The Clergy Review*
*The Life of the Spirit*
*Blackfriars*

# LITURGY AND DOCTRINE

by CHARLES DAVIS                    4s 6d net

". . . it is very valuable reading for all those who wish to understand what the liturgical movement is all about. . . . May it have a multitude of readers. It cannot fail to give light and do good." *The Clergy Review*

"This is one of the most refreshing books I have read in years. There is no member of the English Catholic community who would not benefit from buying it and reading it." *Laurence Bright, O.P., in Life of the Spirit*

"If teachers would study this booklet and use it as a guide in their other reading, we could confidently expect a higher quality of religious teaching."
*F. Somerville, S.J., in The Catholic Teachers Journal*

". . . it is astonishing how much the author gets in in such a small space—but it is so vigorously written that one traverses depths of theology almost without realising it."
*Dom Peter Damien in the Catholic Herald*

". . . an excellent book, probably the best short account in English of the central role of the liturgy in the Christian life." *Doctrine and Life*

# THE RESURRECTION

by F. X. DURRWELL, c.ss.r.　　　　　**30s net**

". . . there is no denying that his work as a whole is a masterpiece; a deeply pondered, beautifully constructed doctrinal synthesis, full of the light and sweetness of a noble intelligence entirely dedicated to the noblest of subject matters . . . it is far too powerful a work not to have a profound effect on speculative theology in the Church for many years to come. It is the kind of book that can alter one's whole view of the subject. From one point of view it is a challenge to the scholastic theology of the Catholic manuals, and one that cannot be ignored."

*Fr. Kenelm Foster, O.P., in Blackfriars*

"This is a most impressive and inspiring piece of work by a French theologian. A brief review cannot hope to do justice to it. . . . This beautifully produced and richly suggestive book may be freely commended to all who hold the faith of the Resurrection." *The British Weekly*

"Anyone who takes an interest in theology, whether priest or layman, specialist or amateur, should find this book exhilarating. The book is quite free from jargon, and indeed both author and translator seem to have avoided many technical expressions which one might have regarded as indispensable. This gives the book a force and directness which no doubt accounts for its powerful impact."

*The Catholic Herald*

# CHRISTIANITY DIVIDED

Edited by D. J. CALLAHAN

Professor OBERMAN and D. J. O'HANLON

For the first time since the fragmentation of Christianity Christians are recognising their essential fellowship. Suspicion and hatred are being replaced by trust and friendship, and we are seriously considering the prospects for reunion. There exist considerable and important doctrinal differences between the Christians of the Roman communion and those of other communions but these are frequently exaggerated by deep misunderstandings, not merely of another's position but often of one's own.

The editors of this book have gathered together some of the finest writing to be found among both Protestant and Catholic theologians. The essays each deal with something central to Christian belief and the results are quite staggering. The writings of **Father Geiselman** and of **Oscar Cullmann** on Scripture will open the eyes of many of us in this country to the way in which we have an immense amount to learn both about our own understanding of Scripture and from that of the great Protestant scholars. **Karl Barth** has an international reputation; what he has to say again is of immense value to Protestants and Romans alike. It is complemented by an essay by the young theologian, **Hans Küng**. There are articles about Christ, the Church, the Sacraments, and two different aspects of Scripture. All these articles are written with a clarity and force only to be found among the great thinkers, either Catholic or Protestant.

Differences are not resolved in this book, but as a result of what is said intelligent and charitable conversation is possible.

**Stagbook 12s 6d net**